BUILDING UNSTOPPABLE TEAMS

BUILDING UNSTOPPABLE TEAMS

*BUSINESS LESSONS INSPIRED BY
THE WORLD'S TOUGHEST CYCLING RACE*

SÉBASTIEN SASSEVILLE
AND GABRIEL RENAUD

Copyright © Sébastien Sasseville and Gabriel Renaud, 2025

Published by ECW Press
665 Gerrard Street East
Toronto, Ontario, Canada M4M 1Y2
416-694-3348 / info@ecwpress.com

All rights reserved. No part of this publication may be reproduced, stored in a retrieval system, or transmitted in any form by any process — electronic, mechanical, photocopying, recording, or otherwise — without the prior written permission of the copyright owners and ECW Press. The scanning, uploading, and distribution of this book via the internet or via any other means without the permission of the publisher is illegal and punishable by law. This book may not be used for text and data mining, AI training, and similar technologies. Please purchase only authorized electronic editions, and do not participate in or encourage electronic piracy of copyrighted materials. Your support of the authors' rights is appreciated.

Editor for the Press: Jennifer Smith
Copy editor: Peter Norman
Cover design: Jessica Albert

PRINTED AND BOUND IN CANADA

ECW Press is a proudly independent, Canadian-owned book publisher. Find out how we make our books better at ecwpress.com/about-our-books.

LIBRARY AND ARCHIVES CANADA CATALOGUING IN PUBLICATION

Title: Building unstoppable teams : business lessons inspired by the world's toughest cycling race / Sébastien Sasseville and Gabriel Renaud.

Other titles: Esprit d'équipe. English

Names: Sasseville, Sébastien, author. | Renaud, Gabriel, author.

Description: Translation of: Esprit d'équipe: se surpasser ensemble dans la course la plus difficile au monde. | In English, translated from the French.

Identifiers: Canadiana (print) 20250139960 | Canadiana (ebook) 20250146835

ISBN 978-1-77041-836-3 (softcover)
ISBN 978-1-77852-414-1 (ePub)
ISBN 978-1-77852-415-8 (PDF)

Subjects: LCSH: Teams in the workplace. | LCSH: Success in business.

Classification: LCC HD66 .S2713 2025 | DDC 658.4/022—dc23

PRINTING: MARQUIS   5 4 3 2 1

This book is printed on FSC®-certified paper. It contains recycled materials, and other controlled sources, is processed chlorine free, and is manufactured using biogas energy.

*To all those who dare to dream big,
and the teams who seek to accomplish the extraordinary.*

CONTENTS

A Word from Sébastien		ix
A Word from Gabriel		xiii
The Race Across America		xvi

PART I BUILDING THE TEAM

Chapter 1	The Mission	3
Chapter 2	Bees and Eagles	8
Chapter 3	Baking the Cake	15
Chapter 4	The Big Reshuffle	23
Chapter 5	The Buy-In	29
Chapter 6	Marginal Gains	42

PART II GENERATING PERFORMANCE

Chapter 7	Going Beyond Your Role	57
Chapter 8	No One Wins Alone	68
Chapter 9	1 + 1 = 11	79
Chapter 10	Breaking in the Bees	91
Chapter 11	Pushing Through Adversity	102
Chapter 12	Rest in Motion	108

PART III ALWAYS MOVING

Chapter 13	Adapt or Die	119
Chapter 14	Hitting the Wall	130
Chapter 15	Making Decisions in Uncertain Times	145
Chapter 16	Final Sprint	152

PART IV CELEBRATING THE JOURNEY

Chapter 17	Small Things Are Big Things	161
Chapter 18	The Finish Line	168
Chapter 19	Honoring the Journey	175
Chapter 20	What's Left of It?	183
Chapter 21	Beyond Engagement, There Is Love	189

Acknowledgments   194

A WORD FROM SÉBASTIEN

All my life, I have wanted my adventures to be useful to others — to be full of meaning, have endless depth and be guided by purpose. More than anything, I want to have an impact.

I'm an ordinary person, but I have always wanted to do something extraordinary. I grew up in a small town, and from my early teens my parents wanted my siblings and I to learn the value of work. I worked on a farm from the age of 13 onwards and initially earned three dollars an hour. Every morning, I rode my bike for a bout three kilometers, rain or shine, and then executed the hardest work I have ever done in my life. Looking back, I realize how formative that experience was and the role it played in developing my resilience and my discipline. This is one of the more meaningful chapters of my life and it had a massive impact on me then, and as I continued to grow.

In 2022, I participated in the Race Across America, the toughest ultra-cycling race in the world. I completed the race in the solo category, which means that I covered the entire distance alone, as opposed to participants who race in relays in teams of two, four or eight cyclists. That said, without the help of my support team, I would never have been able to finish the race, let alone compete as well as I did.

I hope that this book inspires you in your own personal and professional life. In the next few pages, you will meet Gabriel Renaud, the leader of our support team and our crew chief. Gabriel is a dear friend without whom I could never have built such a strong crew, let alone reached my goals with this race.

After Gabriel's short introduction, which comes right after mine, we're going to explain just what the infamous Race Across America is. You'll see how, without a strong logistics support team, it's impossible to even participate, let alone finish, an incredibly grueling course. It's first and foremost this story of collective achievement we want to tell.

You will also get to know the other 10 team members, who watched over me 24 hours a day for the entirety of the race.

I'm an endurance athlete living with type 1 diabetes. I wear an insulin pump that keeps me alive and my condition adds an immense layer of complexity to the athletic challenges I undertake. I hope that my journey will be an inspiration to all those who live with type 1 diabetes. I also hope that my message will have a much wider impact than just on those affected by diabetes. We all face obstacles of our own in our lives, and I hope that you will find insights and motivation in my journey that will be useful in your personal and professional lives.

My athletic pursuits have been quite varied. I've summited Mount Everest and run across Canada, the equivalent of doing 180 marathons in nine months. I've completed 10 Ironman competitions as well as the fabled Sahara Race in the Sahara Desert. In 2021, I made my first foray into the world of ultra-cycling, riding across Canada in less than 16 days. If you are interested in reading about my other adventures, I have detailed them, and most importantly what I have learned from them, in my first book, *One Step at a Time*.[*]

The book you are holding right now addresses the Race Across America exclusively. From the beginning stages of our preparation to the finish line, you will experience the entire story of this incredible adventure.

Building Unstoppable Teams is not just an instruction manual, it is also a philosophy, an ethos.

---

[*] SASSEVILLE, Sébastien. *One Step at a Time: A Tale of Purpose, Resilience, and Determination from Mount Everest to the Sahara*. Tellwell Talent, 2018.

A WORD FROM SÉBASTIEN

Before, during and after the race, an adventure that now spans a few years, Gabriel and I saw and continue to see countless parallels between the Race Across America and business. In fact, this book is primarily written for the business world. This is a guide to build and lead highly engaged and top-performing teams.

If, like many of our readers, you aren't in a leadership position, this book is still for you. If you aspire to build strong relationships, be part of a cohesive team, achieve extraordinary results, get rid of unnecessary tensions and feel a deep connection to a shared mission, our story will provide you with the tools and the fuel to be a better teammate and a positive influence in your team.

Simply put, we all have a role to play in our team's success. We are stronger together, but teamwork doesn't happen by magic. Teamwork is a business strategy and a conscious decision. Therefore, it requires time and effort, resources and planning. Teamwork doesn't make things easier and faster. So why adopt this business strategy? Because when we dream, execute and operate as a team, we can achieve 10 times more.

In our story, we succeeded because we understood, collectively, that even the smallest detail in our preparation and execution was important. Team spirit means giving the best of yourself every day; committing to doing not just a good job but an exceptional one and going beyond our role. That implies that each member of the team is important. You will witness that our team members understood that each of their individual attitudes would get aggregated to create one collective mindset.

Primarily, this experience was a human adventure, and our success depended very much on building strong relationships amongst us. I hope this will be an interesting, inspiring and enriching read. This book is certainly not just about high performance. Personally, through my adventures, I am simply chasing life-changing experiences and memorable moments with people I love. That's true happiness, no matter the outcome.

I also believe that choosing the hardest path, choosing adversity and choosing to do difficult things lead to a richer life. It may be a bit of a cliché, but it really is about the journey. In so choosing, our lives become fulfilled and genuinely happy, regardless of the result. The Race Across America is a challenge that almost no one finishes, so trust me, if you're not in it for the journey, there is no point being there.

You will encounter two voices in this book: Gabriel's and mine. Together, we built and managed a support team that would enable me to reach the finish line. My role was to define our vision and our mission. Gabriel's role as the team's crew chief was taking care of the day-to-day details during the race, which were so critical to our success.

As you can imagine, Gabriel and I had totally different experiences during the race. I spent long hours on my bike, much of which I don't recall well due to extreme exhaustion. I also have a propensity to take a more philosophical outlook on events. Gabriel is usually much more pragmatic and down to earth in his approach. I hope that the dynamic arrangement of these different perspectives will help you better understand the complexities and many different levels to the challenge we undertook.

In my day job I'm a motivational speaker, sharing the knowledge I've gained from my experiences. I get invited to private and public meetings and conferences throughout Canada and the U.S. to speak on teamwork, change management, leadership and building resilience. I'm lucky to collaborate with brilliant individuals from a wide array of backgrounds and work. These exchanges are always enriching for me and, I hope, those I work with. It is through a corporate lens that I often view my athletic pursuits, and you'll see that in our story as well.

You're probably eager to hear about the race, but I'll request a bit of patience. You see, it required six months of preparation for the team to be ready for 12 days of racing. Starting in chapter 7 is when you will live the race in all its minute details. But before that, we're going to tell you the background story, which I promise is equally interesting and important. I knew I was bringing the group to one of the biggest challenges imaginable in sports, so we needed to become a strong team first otherwise we would have never succeeded. In the first half of this book, you will learn how we constructed a high-performance crew and prepared together.

I'd even go as far as to say that the preparation for the race is as grueling and inspiring as the race itself. I hope you'll agree.

A WORD FROM GABRIEL

Since childhood, I have been passionate about sports and performance. It's in my DNA! It began with nights at the outdoor rink, playing hockey until my fingers and toes nearly froze. I continued right up through university, playing NCAA hockey in the United States.

After retiring from hockey, looking for a new challenge, I began Ice Cross Downhill, known globally as Red Bull Crashed Ice. The speed, the adrenaline, the world travel, the camaraderie and friendships — I loved it all. I have so many unforgettable memories from traveling the circuit for six years. My professional sporting career may now be over, but I stay active and take on several smaller athletic challenges every year.

I met Sébastien in 2016. My aunt Marie-Claude, who works at a university in Newfoundland and Labrador, had invited Sébastien to speak at a conference she organized. As soon as she met him, she thought of me and bought me his first book: *One Step at a Time*.

While reading it I fell in love with the simple concept expressed in its title and wanted to meet the author. I reached out, and we met for a coffee, where we had a long chat about our athletic pasts. The fact that Sébastien accepted my invitation says a lot about the individual: humble and approachable in spite of all his accomplishments.

Sébastien was a lesson in humility for me; he taught me to embrace a student's mindset. Being younger at the time, I was impatient and wanted things to happen quickly. I came to realize that by working diligently every day on the right strategic actions, with patience, the results eventually would come on their own. I learned to focus more on the journey rather than the destination.

I also came to realize that it was better to be consistently good rather than occasionally great.

Right around the same time I met Sébastien, I was working as an assistant coach at a school for entrepreneurs near Quebec City. Sébastien came to speak to our students, and those moments together solidified our relationship. We started to collaborate professionally. Eventually, that professional relationship evolved into a true friendship, and we even completed a few athletic challenges together.

It's kind of crazy that I met Sébastien through his first book, and I am now here having written one with him! Anyway, I think it's fantastic, and I'm proud to collaborate with someone who inspires me this much.

Today, I find fulfilment in coaching and helping others reach their goals. I am co-founder of a team-building business, and my obsession is to make teams more engaged, committed, united and successful. This is what I did with our team at the Race Across America, and this is also what you will get out of this book.

The framework provided by the Race Across America proved to be an exceptional laboratory to test my leadership skills. I was able to put into practice all the principles and concepts I use with my clients. Over the next few chapters, you will discover what we put in place to create cohesion and commitment within our team.

During the months of preparation leading up to the Race Across America, we went through all the phases of building a team. First, we pitched the project to candidates and recruited a group of high-potential people. We brought together all team members, most of whom were strangers to each other, and started the process of working towards a common goal. We created cohesion among team members and, most importantly, placed each individual in a position where they could shine by using their talents every day.

A WORD FROM GABRIEL

Our intention with this book is to share our story and what we have learned, with humility. If this book becomes a guide for individuals who aspire to create, build and lead high-performance teams while maintaining strong team cohesion, then we will have achieved our goal. If this book helps you improve and cultivate better relationships on a personal level, it will also have achieved its goal. It can be whatever you want to make of it.

Most of the concepts presented in this book are simple. However, to adopt them, they require a conscious effort, patience and consistency. I like this quote, often attributed to Thomas Edison: "A vision without execution is a hallucination." Common sense is not always common practice. When you put this book down, I humbly invite you to take real and intentional actions on your key takeaways.

Our experience goes beyond the team we assembled and the knowledge we gained from our time together. This group of strangers became more than just a team; we became a family. And that's the outcome we wish for all of your teams.

THE RACE ACROSS AMERICA

Gabriel Renaud

The Race Across America (RAAM), unlike the Tour de France, is not a bicycle race in stages. Rather, it is a single-stage, continuous time trial over 4,800 kilometers. When the clock starts, it never stops, even when you stop to sleep.

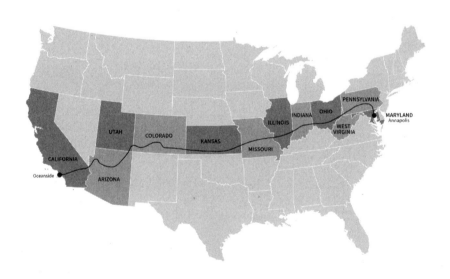

Route of the 2022 Race Across America.

THE RACE ACROSS AMERICA

The race starts in Oceanside, California, and ends in Annapolis, Maryland, with a few variations to the location of the start and finish lines since the first edition of the race in 1982. The route crosses the United States from west to east, as well as several types of terrain: desert, mountains, rainforests, plains and valleys.

If you aren't a cyclist, and even then, there is a good chance you've never heard of this race. While it's been held for over 40 years by an extremely well ran, administrated and managed organization, the event hasn't quite made it into popular culture and mainstream media. To many ultra cycling purists, it would kill the race spirit if it would become more popular.

The race does not take place on a closed circuit. This means that cyclists must share the road with motorists and obey the local traffic rules. For example, if the light is red, the cyclist must stop and wait for the green light or face a penalty. Each team must also obey a long list of rules (a 60-page document) or again, face a penalty. Minor penalties result in additional time at the finish; major penalties result in disqualification from the race.

In 2022, only 35 athletes were registered in the solo category. (It is also possible to participate in RAAM as a team of two, four or eight people.) To participate in the solo category, the main event, athletes must be invited to, or qualify through, one of the official ultra-cycling qualifying races. Basically, aspirants must demonstrate that they can ride at an average of 16.8 km/h, including sleep periods, for a distance of more than 560 kilometers. That said, ultra-cycling races are rarely under 800 kilometers. Sébastien earned his qualifying ticket through his crossing of Canada the previous year, a 6,000-kilometre ride that he completed in 15 days and 17 hours.

What makes RAAM so special is that participants must complete the race in a maximum of 12 days. This means that the slowest a cyclist can go is 400 kilometers per day, 12 days straight. In order to complete the distance within the time limit, athletes typically sleep only two to three hours a day for the entire race. This extreme sleep deprivation is certainly the greatest challenge of RAAM.

Lack of sleep also affects the cyclists' support team, which usually consists of six to 10 people. Although the support team sleeps more than the cyclist, the hours are still limited and not always of the best quality.

The support team includes drivers, navigators, cooks, mechanics, photographers and videographers, health specialists, media specialists and a crew chief.

The cyclists, with their teams, have the right to use any strategy they wish. They can decide not to sleep for the first 48 hours to cover as many kilometers as possible. Alternatively, they can choose a conservative strategy and sleep 4 hours in the first 24. They can choose to sleep during the day, or at night, in a hotel, or on the side of the road on a floor mat. It's up to each team, but regardless of strategy, this race is a great operational challenge.

Depending on the strategy and the budget available, the choice of vehicles is different for each team. Some teams will focus on agility and will opt for three smaller vehicles such as minivans or sprinters. Other teams will focus on comfort and opt for a larger recreational vehicle.

Throughout the course, there are 54 time stations. Each time station is a checkpoint that brings you closer to the finish. At each time station, the team must check in on the race web portal. This allows the organizers to follow the progress of each cyclist. Each cyclist is also equipped with a GPS tracker, which provides their position in real time on the official RAAM website. This feature, referred to as "dot watching" in the RAAM community, is greatly appreciated by family and friends who follow their loved one's progress from home. It can also become quite addictive!

You could say that RAAM is a relatively simple bicycle race, with the goal of getting your cyclist from point A to point B. However, it's a whole other challenge to do so with the operational complexity of operating three vehicles simultaneously, covering around 500 kilometers per day, complying with a long list of regulations, and having to feed a team of 10 people. Added to this complexity are the elements of nature beyond our control: the extreme heat of the desert, the slope of the mountains and the strong winds of the plains. Each team must also deal with its share of unforeseen events: mechanical breakdowns, navigation errors, falls, dehydration, conflicts within the team and, for us, the management of Sébastien's diabetes.

All of these elements make this the toughest ultra-cycling race in the world. More people summit Mount Everest every year than there have been RAAM finishers in 40 years. The race is 50 percent longer than the Tour de France, and participants must complete it in half the time.

In 2022, the year of our participation, less than 50 percent of solo athletes finished the race.

RAAM is a beast; RAAM is a monster. It is an event to be taken seriously. No amount of determination can replace proper preparation. Without a well-trained support team, the best cyclist in the world could not last more than 24 hours.

The only way to defeat the beast is to attack it together.

PART I

BUILDING THE TEAM

To build a strong team, you must view someone else's strength as a complement to your weakness and not as a threat to your position or authority.

— CHRISTINE CAINE,
AUTHOR AND PUBLIC SPEAKER

CHAPTER 1

THE MISSION

Sébastien Sasseville

No matter how good the carpenter, a house won't stand for long without a solid foundation. Before involving others in a challenge as extreme as RAAM, I needed a solid understanding of why I was undertaking it: to challenge myself, obviously. But beyond that? What was my real and intrinsic motivation for RAAM?

The experiences I had through several other high-endurance sporting challenges prior to RAAM had shown me that the core reason we do what we do — our WHY — is what is ultimately the most powerful fuel.

This idea has been widely popularized in the last decade, notably by Simon Sinek.[*] All organizations and leaders agree that a strong WHY is the basis for success and resilience. Therefore, a team with a strong and shared WHY is a strong and resilient team. That said, you may have heard the concept of the WHY many times already. It's not entirely wrong to say that the term has become overused in our organizations, diminishing its impact.

I would also argue that sometimes, purpose is not enough. When former NFL quarterback Tom Brady was on the field facing 11 other big and strong athletes who just wanted to go through him, I'm quite certain he did not

---

[*] SINEK, Simon. *Start with Why: How Great Leaders Inspire Everyone to Take Action*. Portfolio, 2011.

think about his kids at that time. Sometimes, grit is the only answer. More specifically, an extreme and completely devoted focus on the next task.

I much prefer the word *mission*. It evokes not only a goal that needs to be achieved, but also the importance of achieving it. A mission suggests an impact that is bigger than us, greater than the task itself.

So what is my mission?

My mission is to inspire people to set big goals and help them take the first step to achieve things they didn't think were possible.

My journey is not about overcoming obstacles. Rather, it's about *choosing* them. By choosing to do difficult things, I have realized that my resilience grows and allows me to accomplish greater and greater things. When we consistently choose to do difficult things, ultimately what we conceive possible expands, and that is an incredible gift. This is what I wanted to show through my journey in RAAM.

Ultimately, my mission is also about transformation and improvement. Ultra events offer the guarantee that you will learn and be transformed at the end. You just don't always know how, and I find that incredibly exciting. The hardest endurance events are a different type of teacher. It isn't you that is looking for something, but rather what you need to learn that will find you.

Now, how do you recruit 10 people for a project that is not theirs? How do you convince people to give so much of their time for a year? And above all, how do you make sure that all these people are not merely present, but that they also give their best from beginning to end?

The answer is the mission. The role of the leader is not to tell the team what to do. The leader gives the team something to believe in: the mission. Leaders provide meaning. In order to succeed, the team must develop a deep emotional connection to the mission. The mission dictates our mindset, actions and behaviors. When the mission is understood, it is so much easier to embrace change and to accept to change the how, so we continue to serve the mission.

Here's how I defined the mission of our participation at RAAM: to inspire people with type 1 diabetes to believe that there is no limit to what they can accomplish despite the disease. In short, I wanted to do good by helping people with type 1 diabetes think big and not let their condition get in the way of their accomplishing their dreams.

With the mission in hand, I also had a specific goal to create a transformative life experience for each team member. I knew we were going to have a deeply human experience, from which I wanted them to grow. It's impossible not to be transformed by such a challenge, so I knew the opportunity for growth that the race presented would help me with recruitment.

RAAM was going to be so much more than a bike race. I knew it would be the experience of a lifetime for the whole team.

To complete RAAM in the solo category, a cyclist needs support to ride 21 hours a day, making it a very complex logistical challenge. The team must first invest hundreds of hours in their preparation over the course of the year prior to the race.

To add to the complication, each team member had to use two weeks of their precious vacation time for the actual race. These people were mostly volunteers, friends and family who had day jobs and lives outside of RAAM.

Creating an unforgettable experience for each team member meant offering them an opportunity to grow, learn and develop both personally and professionally. I didn't want to ask for help or beg for support. As a leader, I wanted to create an opportunity impossible to refuse. I believe that leaders make the future brighter. Leaders create an improved future reality for everyone on their team.

The road ahead would certainly be fraught with challenges. Leaders choose adversity and don't shy away from big tests, oppositely they lean into the obstacle. As J.A. Hadfield so brilliantly said, *"if only we fearlessly accept the challenge and confidently expend our strength, every danger or difficulty brings its own strength."*[*] Personally, I don't believe that people become demotivated and disengaged because the challenge is too difficult. In fact, the research shows opposite to be true — if the challenge is too small, it doesn't excite people, and their intrinsic motivation decreases.[**]

People want to contribute to something that is meaningful and changes the world. No matter how big or small the challenge, people

---

[*] HADFIELD, J.A. *The Psychology of Power.* New York: The Macmillan Co., 1919.

[**] ABUHAMDEH, Sami, and CSIKSZENTMIHALYI, Mihaly. The Importance of Challenge for the Enjoyment of Intrinsically Motivated, Goal-Directed Activities. *Personality and Social Psychology Bulletin*, 2012, vol. 38, no. 3, pp. 317-330.

want to feel like they are doing important, impactful work. Don't be afraid of big goals, even ones that seem impossible; sometimes it's the best way to attract top talent.

THE SUM OF OUR STRENGTHS

One of my first tasks was to present the project to the people I was trying to recruit. I immediately impressed upon them that I was confident we could be successful together.

Before accepting, some team members confessed to suffering from imposter syndrome. Why choose me for this team? Am I adequate? Do I have sufficient experience? Will I be good enough? I had no doubts that they were right for the job and told them so. I was sincere and had known each of these individuals personally for many years. (In the next chapter, I will discuss how I chose each individual and why I knew they were the right players.)

Individually, they saw their shortcomings and their point of weakness. From my vantage point, I could see the sum of all their strengths. That's the power of a team: a group of people whose combined strengths offset individual weaknesses. When put together, these individuals were a team with all the skills we needed to succeed.

Already, at this early stage, the groundwork for that greater future I mentioned a moment ago was being laid. They began to believe that yes, they could — no, should — be part of this team that would accomplish something remarkable.

EMBODYING THE MISSION

The challenge of the race itself certainly piqued curiosity, but it was the broader mission that convinced each team member to jump into the adventure. A mission that was to help others help themselves, diabetics or not, to dream big, to take a first step. My commitment to this mission was embodied in all my athletic accomplishments since my diagnosis of type 1 diabetes in 2002. Everybody felt, saw and understood my commitment. A mission must go beyond good intentions — it must be lived.

This is critical because we all have an infallible radar for detecting self-interested missions. And here you only get one shot. As soon as people detect that the mission is for the leader's own advancement, people immediately jump off the boat.

The mission must be for the common good, for the service of others. I must mention that there is nothing wrong with benefiting personally from taking part in a mission. For example, a company makes a profit if its mission is accomplished, and there's nothing wrong with that. In fact, that's what we hope.

Along with a powerful mission, I believe that each team member also saw how they would personally advance and grow from this adventure and their commitment. That combo always makes for strong engagement.

But the profit, in whatever form it takes, is a consequence of the mission, not its main objective. We must always serve the mission first. It serves as a beacon and guides all our decisions and behaviors.[*] Ultimately, once the mission is accomplished, the profit will be there and each team member will have benefited from the experience.

The foundation of a strong team is its mission, and it's the leader's responsibility to embody this mission in all their daily actions, decisions and behaviors.

Strong leaders aren't made in grand isolated gestures. The leaders we want to follow embody the mission in *all* their actions, even the most trivial. True leadership resides in coherence and in the consistency between the mission and all our actions.

---

[*] IRELAND, R. Duane, and HIRC, Michael A. Mission Statements: Importance, Challenge, and Recommendations for Development. *Business Horizons*, 1992, vol. 35, no. 3, pp. 34-42.

CHAPTER 2

BEES AND EAGLES

Sébastien Sasseville

I am monopolizing the first few chapters of this book for a simple reason. When the race began on June 14, 2022, my "vacation" also began. Once I crossed the starting line, my job became extremely simple: pedal, eat and sleep.

But one thing was extremely clear. If we were to succeed, the team would get all the credit. If we failed to reach the finish line in time, I would be accountable. Since during the race my role would be of an athlete and not a leader, I knew I needed to build an autonomous team and a team of experts. The higher we go in influence and leadership, the more we will be judged on our team's performance, rather than our individual results. Whenever I see a leader who's too busy to spend time with their team, because they have been sucked into the operations or other tasks for example, it tells me that this leader doesn't understand what their role truly is.

A year before the start, I made a wish and a commitment to fully and completely surrender to the team during the race. The team would then be 100 percent in charge, and they would make all the decisions. They would tell me what to do and when to do it: what to eat, what to wear, when to stop, when to continue, when to sleep. During the race, my job would be to listen to them.

I challenged myself to create a dream team. Even though we were all going to be rookies at RAAM, I had the belief that with hard work and effort, we would have a team that would provide me with superior logistical support. I would be sandbagging if I said that I'm not a good athlete. I'm obviously fitter than the average joe. But the reality is, I have never won a race, and compared to the top cyclists, I am average. I had a vision where the support team would be my advantage.

I am a dreamer who brings people together. Gabriel is organized, disciplined and has a natural talent for operations. He is also an expert in fostering collaboration within organizations, helping companies develop strong and collaborative cultures to drive results. For months, Gabriel's leadership and knowledge were an essential part of our weekly team meetings.

Ironically, Gabriel was the one who thought the longest before deciding to join the team. Some team members agreed instantly. Most took a week to think about it, discuss the project with their partners and quickly came back to me with a yes. Gabriel didn't. He took more than a month to decide. It got to the point where I wondered if he really wanted a part of this! I held out because I knew he was the leader I needed.

Once Gabriel was on board, I figured out why he took so long. Gabriel takes his commitments very seriously. For him, when one commits, it is only to give the best of oneself. He needed to take the time to evaluate how he would benefit from it in his personal and professional life. Before saying yes, he wanted to make sure that he could do the project with the dedication it deserved.

In my opinion, Gabriel's involvement will always remain one of the keys to our success. Then, if I had to pinpoint my biggest contribution, it was my selection of the other team members. After all, while Gabriel was taking his time thinking about whether or not to join, I had to keep the project moving!

Bees and eagles. It's a principle I developed after my first ultra-cycling experience, my failed attempt to break the Guinness record for the fastest crossing of Canada on a bike.

Picture it. The image says it all. In a team, you need the right proportion of eagles to bees. Furthermore, eagles and bees should not try to fill each other's roles.

An eagle isn't necessarily a leader. An eagle is an individual with a strategic vision. An eagle doesn't waste energy, it observes from on high and doesn't dive often. But when it does, it is for an essential tactical intervention. The eagle likes to think, to prepare, to anticipate obstacles. The eagle understands the political game and the different players in the ecosystem.

The eagle does not act in the heat of the moment. From its elevated height, the eagle is focused on devising an efficient plan of attack. However, unfortunately, at times, this focus on strategic thinking can hinder the execution on the ground.

That's why a team also needs bees. The bee is industrious, foraging every day. The bee is a go-getter, hard-working, with total commitment to its particular role. When the bee sees a problem, it doesn't hesitate and jumps in. The bee is tireless, does not complain and does whatever it takes to complete a task.

The bee doesn't always see the big picture; sometimes it needs to be reminded of the impact of its role on the overall team and project. The bee is in the moment, so it needs help to understand that its current actions must support the larger mission.

Self-awareness is crucial. When the eagle tries to be a bee, it can turn into micro-management. With their narrower focus, bees should not try to be eagles. And eagles must let the bees work! Trust becomes important. When the eagles try to help the bees, they get in the way and slow down the execution. The bees don't always take the best path as seen by the eagle. The bee, on the other hand, is in the frenzy of reality, so done is better than perfect. The bee is always adapting and adjusting at high speed to reach its goals despite its apparent imperfections.

In turn, the bees need to understand that while the eagle may not look like it is working hard as it hovers calmly at high altitude, its strategic contribution is indispensable. The eagle ensures that the team is moving in the right direction, anticipating dangers and accomplishing its mission.

It's quite simple, and we've all seen it. A team with too many bees can work extremely hard, but they can burn themselves out and fail to reach their goal because they weren't chasing the right thing. Too many eagles, and you'll never take real concrete action to make progress. The outcome won't be any better.

There is no magic formula or ideal bee-to-eagle ratio. It is the nature of the objective that determines the right ratio of eagles to bees. A project can be divided into different phases, during which more eagles or more bees may be needed at any given time.

When I tried to set the record for the fastest crossing of Canada by bike, I made it from Vancouver to Halifax in 15 days and 17 hours. Not a record, but still not an embarrassing performance. Due to lack of experience, we made several costly logistical mistakes. My support team was far too small; we didn't have the right vehicles and didn't have the required expertise within the team. But, most of all, as the team's leader, I made the mistake of choosing too many eagles.

In the case of an ultra-cycling event, an effective support team is composed mainly of bees. When I crossed Canada, I chose close friends, people I thought were brilliant — which they were. I then found myself on the ground with a team of eagles who, when the time came to act, execute, adapt and solve problems, were in their heads way too much. They had a lot of strategic vision, but they were people who looked at each other wondering what to do. I did have some bees on the team, but not enough. As a result, the entire workload fell on their shoulders, and they burned out.

With this learning in mind, a year before the start of RAAM, I began building the team. First, I listed the skills and expertise needed. This time, I was going to recruit based on our objective, not friendships.

THE MISSION IS THE REAL EMPLOYER

I identified the personality traits that were essential to the success of our mission. Indomitability and a "whatever it takes" attitude were going to be important traits, but the top of the list: no ego.

I knew we would have to operate in a difficult environment, sleep-deprived and with daily contingencies. I wanted a harmonious team with no conflict. After all, we were going to do a bike race; we are not heart surgeons, nor are we going on a humanitarian mission.

A team of 11 people is large enough for conflicts to happen. In fact, a team of two can do it. No ego means understanding the interdependence of each other's roles, which means understanding that all roles are equally important. It means that the good and the bad belong to the whole team. Successes and failures are shared. No ego means openness to the other, to different ideas. It means that no one wants to win an argument; we want to find the best solution together, to serve our shared goal. It means boundless humility, an ability to admit mistakes and ask for help.

Ultimately, no ego in the team means that the mission is the real employer. No ego means each member is serving the mission first rather than protecting their role. Nothing was more important to me. I was going to be uncompromising in that regard. I would not accept any conflict due to a clash of egos. None whatsoever.

Of course, friction is certainly possible, but conflict and friction are different. Trust me, not all our discussions were always harmonious! Friction is normal and can be caused by adrenaline, lack of sleep or a high-pressure environment — that's fine with me. But I was going to be intransigent on this; friction and conflict could never take roots in ego. (To learn more about healthy friction in the workplace, I recommend Tim Arnold's excellent book *The Power of Healthy Tension*.)[*]

Once I determined the expertise and personality types needed, I began recruiting. One of my good friends, a logistics expert, would have been an ideal candidate. Ideal, except that he has a very strong ego, and I knew he would want to be the "boss." Consequently, I ruled him out, even though from a technical perspective he was probably the best.

Another extremely valuable friend I admire was on my list. Unfortunately, thinking further I realized that he is an eagle, so I had to leave him off. These choices weren't easy, but it was my responsibility to make rational choices aligned with our goal.

PERSONALITY OVER SKILL

You have to observe the individuals in real life to be sure if you are dealing with an eagle or a bee. The people I chose were not all my close friends, but they were at least acquaintances I had observed over the past few years.

---

[*] ARNOLD, Tim. *The Power of Healthy Tension: Overcome Chronic Issues and Conflicting Values.* HRD Press, 2017.

For example, Marc-Antoine was part of the support team during the cross-Canada record attempt. As a videographer, his role was to capture the adventure. I was able to witness his immense talent, but also his energy, tenacity and incredible dedication to the mission. He was totally committed to his role. In fact, he almost didn't sleep during the trip because he was filming during the day and editing at night. This devotion to his work really impressed and inspired me.

I also wanted my brother-in-law, Martin, to join our team. I knew that Martin would be a key player, so much so that I had asked him to join us in 2021 for the crossing of Canada. He refused and later told me that he was afraid to disappoint, not knowing if he would have enough time to prepare for his role. Martin likes things to be planned and done to perfection. I have seen him tinker, repair and build just about everything in his house; I knew he was meticulous, passionate and a perfectionist. These were skills I needed on the team.

The same goes for Valérie, Gabriel's partner, who joined the team as our social network manager. Her professionalism is striking, and all our professional interactions before her involvement in RAAM convinced me that she would be perfect. It was her reliability and the fact that she always delivered on all her promises (and more) that built trust. Another bee I could delegate to with confidence, and then forget these tasks with the assurance that everything would be done, perfectly and on time. Every manager's dream!

When recruiting and looking at resumes, we tend to look for the accomplishments of candidates. We see numbers, jobs, roles held. What we need to do instead is look for behaviors, mindset, qualities and values that are aligned with the culture of our organization and our goals.*

Before talking about the project and starting to recruit, I made a list of qualities that would be important for the success of the mission. Hardworking, reliable, adaptable, tenacious and open-minded. At first glance, these are qualities that all employers want in their employees.

But when you get right down to it, these qualities are essential for an event like RAAM. The support team was going to have to be in operation

---

* BOWEN, David E., LEDFORD JR., Gerald E., and NATHAN, Barry R. Hiring for the Organization, Not the Job. *Academy of Management Perspectives*, 1991, vol. 5, no. 4, 35-51.

24 hours a day, working very hard in difficult weather conditions, dealing with unforeseen circumstances every day and ensuring my safety and performance no matter the situation.

When recruiting, look for qualities and personality traits, not accomplishments.

One teammate at a time, one bee at a time, the team formed. With each addition, I kept in mind my commitment to surrender to the team starting June 14. To just pedal and trust them with all decisions.

For me, trust is neither given nor earned, it is cultivated. Trust is an outcome. Trust is built in all the little daily gestures, not in the big moves. Trust is created when we overdeliver on a thousand micro-commitments.

Trust also can't be an expectation of perfection. Think of a time when you needed something important done. You went to your top performer and told them, "I trust you." What that truly meant is: "Don't mess this up!" Trust should be comforting. It's a dance, it requires two people and a commitment to provide a best effort on one part, and a promise to support on the other.

As team leader, I knew we had something special. The sum of everyone's expertise, personalities and strengths had the makings of a team I had dreamed of. The only problem was that I was the only one who knew.

I knew every member of the team personally, but they were mostly unknown to each other. We were going to have to go from 11 strangers to one team.

For Gabriel and me, building that team was a bit like making a cake together. I can take some credit for choosing the perfect ingredients. Gabriel then took those ingredients and, with his special recipe and exceptional leadership skills, baked a memorable cake.

CHAPTER 3

BAKING THE CAKE

Gabriel Renaud

If I took a long time to make my decision to join this adventure, it was because I wanted to ensure that I could invest myself 100 percent, both personally and professionally. On the personal side, I wanted to see if participating in RAAM was something that interested my partner, Valérie. I knew that RAAM was exactly the kind of life experience I look for, and I felt that living this experience as a couple would make it even more enriching and unforgettable. Happily, Valérie didn't take long to make her decision. She's the kind of person who goes for it. "If you want to do it, I'll go with you!"

On the professional side, the decision was far more difficult, as committing to RAAM meant putting less time into my business for a while. However, the opportunity was too good to turn down. Plus, Sébastien gave me carte blanche and trusted me 100 percent to implement whatever I wanted within the team. This would be an exceptional laboratory! It was the perfect playground to test, implement and improve the many principles that make a team successful.

Sébastien already had a vision in mind and, whether or not I knew it yet, I was part of it. I remember one dinner at my house when he kept telling me what a *dream team* we had. I loved his enthusiasm, but it was just intuition that hadn't yet been proven. He talked about bees and eagles, a principle I found quite interesting, but I wanted to test and validate his instincts. Did the team really have the natural strengths that a challenge like RAAM required?

THE SIX TYPES OF WORKING GENIUS

I was joining a team that was already formed and whose members I didn't know. This is often the case in the workplace, where managers can't always choose all their team members. At this point, the most important thing for me was to see if we had the right players in place for the challenge ahead.

I suggested to Sébastien that we put the team through the Six Types of Working Genius assessment developed by Patrick Lencioni.[*] This is a powerful self-awareness tool that helps to map a team's strengths and weaknesses.

I wanted to determine the areas of genius of each team member and see if their talents matched the demands of the challenge. The more I read about RAAM, the more I realized that we needed mostly operational people who weren't afraid to get their hands dirty. In other words, we needed a team of bees.

Lencioni's assessment gives us a ranking in order from the strongest to the weakest of the six geniuses of each individual. Positions one and two are areas of genius, positions three and four are areas of competence and positions five and six are areas of frustration.

The areas of genius refers to the intersection of our abilities and passions. It is a zone where the individual is naturally gifted and finds joy and energy in what they do. An individual should spend as much time as possible in their areas of genius. Under these conditions, individuals are engaged and contribute to the mission to the best of their ability. When people are working in their areas of genius, the benefits to the organization are immense. These employees want to contribute more, without counting their hours; they act out of passion, commitment and a burning desire to succeed.

---

[*] LENCIONI, Patrick. *6 Types of Working Genius: A Better Way to Understand Your Gifts, Your Frustrations, and Your Team.* Matt Holt Books, 2022.

The competence zone denotes the tasks for which we have the skills, but about which we are not particularly passionate. You want to be careful with the competence zone because you can become a reference point for your team for certain skills and tasks, without wanting to be one. Many burnouts originate in the competence zone: you become recognized for something that gives you little joy and prevents you from spending time in your areas of genius.

The zone of frustration refers to that area we are neither talented nor passionate about. It is a zone to avoid at all costs. When an individual is required to do work in their frustration zone, they will often feel guilt, incompetence and inefficient because they are not up to the task. For the same task, it will often take four hours for the person in their competence zone, whereas it will take one for the person in their zone of genius.

Using the six-genius test would allow us to create a team map and establish where our collective strengths and weaknesses lay. Finally, this test would allow us to recruit the few missing pieces to the team, if any adjustment was needed.

Here are the definitions of the Six Types of Working Genius. Note that I've shortened them from Lencioni's original work:

Wonder: People with the Genius of Wonder love to speculate and question. They ask questions like, "Why are things the way they are? Is there a better way?"

Invention: People with the Genius of Invention get joy from taking on challenges and generating solutions. They enjoy innovating from scratch and love a blank whiteboard on which they can brainstorm.

Discernment: People with the Genius of Discernment have a natural ability to evaluate the workability of ideas. They know how to connect the dots and give people good feedback across a broad range of topics.

Galvanizing: People with the Genius of Galvanizing love to get things moving. They are great at pushing people out of their comfort zone and inspiring them to get started.

Enablement: People with the Genius of Enablement make things happen. They know how to help, when to help, and can flex to whatever the situation calls for.

Tenacity: People with the Genius of Tenacity are task-oriented and love to take things across the finish line. They ensure a project is going to have the impact it's supposed to have and lives up to agreed-upon standards.

Naturally, you may have guessed that the Geniuses of Wonder, Invention, Discernment and Galvanizing are eagle characteristics. These encompass higher-order strategic thinkers important to the planning stages of a project. The Enablement and Tenacity types correlate with bee characteristics. These are lower-altitude tactical geniuses that contribute during the execution stages of the project.

When I saw our team's results, I was excited! Out of a team of 11 people, we had seven bees, one eagle and three hybrids, including Sébastien. Not only did that meet the needs of the challenge ahead, but our eagle was already in the eagle role, and our hybrids were in hybrid roles. The six bees were our operations people who would have their noses deep in the action.

The way Sébastien built this team is a good example of an individual in his zone of genius. Sébastien, who possesses the Genius of Galvanizing, was successful at recruiting, and naturally recruited the right individuals for the mission.

What would I have done if the test had revealed that our bees had been eagles? Since the individuals had already been recruited and Sébastien already had a relationship with them, a first option would have been to move forward with these individuals knowing that we were not positioned to succeed. By consciously deciding to do so, we would have had to expend more energy to achieve the same result. We would have had much lower engagement and a sentiment of being fulfilled in our roles, and to be frank, our chances of success would be lower too.

The second option would have been to make staffing changes. That's why it's ideal to do this kind of testing in conjunction with recruitment, not after.

Once I had a picture of our team, I had two observations. The first was that we had two geniuses that were well represented in the team: Enablement and Tenacity. My second observation was diversity amongst the team.

When Enablement is well represented in the team, there is a constant desire to help and provide the necessary support for the implementation

RAAM 2022 TEAM MAP

WONDER		INVENTION	
Genius	**Frustration**	**Genius**	**Frustration**
Daniel Marc-Antoine	Gabriel Manon Martin Valérie Marie-Michele Réjean	Marc-Antoine Philippe	Gabriel Manon Orphé Valérie

DISCERNMENT		GALVINIZING	
Genius	**Frustration**	**Genius**	**Frustration**
	Sébastien Philippe	Sébastien Valérie Philippe	Daniel Martin Orphe Marie-Michéle Réjean

ENABLEMENT		TENACITY	
Genius	**Frustration**	**Genius**	**Frustration**
Daniel Gabriel Manon Martin Orphe Valérie Marie-Michele Réjean	Marc-Antoine Sébastien	Gabriel Manon Martin Orphe Sébastien Marie-Michéle Réjean	Daniel Marc-Antoine Philippe

Portrait of our team by genius. Each individual's name appears four times (twice for the genius area and twice for the frustration area). The competency zone is left out. The left column represents the individuals who possess the genius. The right column represents the individuals, for whom, the genius is an area of frustration.

of the project. This was essential for our mission. RAAM was to be a supporter-centric challenge; we would have to be there for Sébastien's needs 24/7!

When Tenacity is well represented in a team, the team is a lot more likely to meet its goals since it will persevere to the finish line. Again, this was totally aligned with the challenges we would experience at RAAM. It would be hard for Sébastien to give up with a team as tenacious as ours!

With respect to diversity, there were several character types. For example, if we needed to be more strategic or to generate new ideas for problems we faced, I could turn to Marc-Antoine, Philippe or Dan. If I needed someone to give a talk to bring us together, I could count on Philippe or Valérie. In short, there were many complementary strengths in the team.

Sébastien had done an excellent job of recruiting. With this assessment, we confirmed that we had the right players sitting in the right chairs. Now I was confident that we could move forward and succeed.

ONBOARDING INDIVIDUALS

My next priority was to onboard individuals. When you have a new guest for dinner, you want everything to be perfect. You clean your home and cook a good meal. Similarly, when you bring in a new employee, you take the time to do an onboarding meeting to discuss the culture and values of the team.

So, to that end, I met with each individual to further integrate them into the team. The objective was to get to know them, to understand their motivations and to make sure they understood the scope of the challenge they were embarking on.

Sébastien had told me repeatedly that his goal was to surrender to the team. This meant that as of June 14, the team would become Sébastien's brain. All decisions, no matter how difficult, including managing his diabetes, would fall into our hands. This was a great vote of confidence from Sébastien to the team, but it came with an even greater responsibility: be accountable at all times. I wanted everyone on the team to understand what was at stake.

Sébastien was first of all a close friend, and I was aware that RAAM was a dangerous challenge. If road cycling by itself can be a dangerous sport, imagine the risks of sleep deprivation over multiple consecutive days. In addition, RAAM passes through a few highways where the speed limit goes up to 100 km/h. On these highways, cyclists must cross several exits and access roads, which in my opinion is the most dangerous part of RAAM.

Sadly, fatalities are no stranger to the race. In 40 years of racing, three cyclists have been fatally struck. Each year, RAAM also sees falls and accidental contact with motorists that lead to withdrawals.

RAAM was to be taken as seriously as a Mount Everest expedition. The risks were real, and I wanted all team members to understand the magnitude of our responsibility. It's one thing to accept an invitation from a friend to travel across the United States. It's another thing to understand and seriously commit to the preparatory steps I had in mind: weekly meetings, team-building exercises, team dinners, a dress rehearsal and three days of final preparation before the race started. There would be no half measures, and if there were members who were not sure they wanted to fully commit to the project, there was still time to change their minds.

I had a one-hour meeting with each member of our team. Understanding their motivation allowed me as a leader to adapt my approach to each individual. Since this was a voluntary project, I assumed that everyone was intrinsically motivated and involved for the right reasons.

These first individual meetings were greatly appreciated by team members. It allowed us to establish points of connection which would enable us to start conversations and build our relationships with one another.

Connection points refer to the commonalities you discover when you meet a new person.[*] For example, with Philippe, one of the connection points was that we are both entrepreneurs. With Marie-Michèle, it was that she works in the clinic where I was treated for my sports injuries. Orphé, like me, is passionate about the history of World War II. These points of connection were important in building trusting relationships.

Looking back, I believe that the one-on-one exercise was thought-provoking for many team members. Sometimes, the result was unexpected. As proof of the relevance and impact of these meetings, two members of the team announced a few weeks later that they were leaving the adventure.

Departures are inevitable when you impose elevated standards of engagement. Clearly communicating expectations makes it easier for individuals to decide if they want to be part of the journey. People leaving your team can be a blessing. It's better to have departures at the beginning of a project than carrying unengaged individuals who drag down the organization.

I was sad to hear of their departure, because they were people with whom I had had good connections. With five months to go before the

---

[*] CHALIFOUX, Benoit. *Being Your Best: The Incredible Power of Relationship Skills*. Édito, 2020.

race, we found ourselves with two players missing. We had to replace them quickly, which also meant that we would have to integrate two strangers into a team that was already starting to form its bonds.

CHAPTER 4

THE BIG RESHUFFLE

Sébastien Sasseville

The two team members who decided to leave us were not just any two. They were two of my best friends — friendships that have lasted for over 20 years.

Six months earlier, I had invited them to jump into the adventure. I knew they were no bees, but I figured that going on this trip with them would make our friendship grow even more. Now that we were in our early forties, with our lives a little more settled, they accepted, figuring that the journey was a once-in-a-lifetime opportunity.

After a few weeks, these two friends withdrew from the project, and thank goodness they did, because today our friendship is still intact. In chapter 2, I recommended recruiting by looking for personality traits, not accomplishments or relationships. This method will inevitably present you with some difficult choices. When you're faced with a candidate who at first glance is outstanding, a pearl, has a rock-solid CV and an impressive track record, but who does not have the required personality, what should you do? I was faced with this exact scenario, and I made the mistake of choosing them.

The reasons my friends gave for leaving were that the workload was too great given their family and professional obligations. They also felt a lack of connection to the mission. Also, the idea of having to perform for 12 days with very little sleep was intimidating. They doubted that they had the energy and fitness for such a challenge.

It was the seriousness of our approach that allowed these players to realize the size of the commitment required. They not only grasped that they were not in the right place, but they had the courage to communicate it. Once the first friend withdrew from the project, the other one followed, as they basically wanted to experience it together.

Initially, this caused us trouble because we had to find at least one replacement. But this had nothing to do with them; the mistake was all mine. I had deviated from the plan and chosen eagles. I had chosen people I really liked, but who were not the right candidates for the mission.

In a business context, this is a very costly mistake. Bad hires turn into unhappy, non-performing employees. When these employees remain in the organization, missions and goals are not met. The overall cost of a termination is also enormous. By overall cost, I mean a financial cost, but also time, impact on team morale and the like.

In the context of a voluntary involvement, it was irrelevant to try to put a number on the loss. Nevertheless, the risk to the mission was still considerable. Gabriel and I knew we were losing two good players. After all, bees without eagles don't go very far. We also feared a negative impact on the rest of the team, as it brought some uncertainty into the mix.

POSITIVISM, IN EVERYTHING, EVERY DAY AND ALWAYS

In a difficult situation, Gabriel and I always look for the positive and for the lesson learned. So how could we turn this situation into a positive event and something that would make the team stronger?

Our reflection began. I then remembered a quote I heard at a conference: "When we hire, a *culture fit is great, but a culture add is even better.*" This was the way to turn this loss into a positive. What are we losing that we need to replace, and what does the team not have that we need to find?

Looking at the glass half empty, we could have asked ourselves questions like: "We are going from 10 to eight people, are we going to make it?" "Did we do something wrong to make them leave?" Looking at the glass half full, we asked ourselves questions like: "How can we use this opportunity to improve our situation?" Positivism, in everything, always and every day, is a quality that makes you want to follow someone. For leaders, optimism isn't a nice-to-have, optimism *is* the job.

We were losing some wisdom, two eagles. Importantly, we immediately communicated with the rest of the team that two of our teammates were leaving. We refused to frame this like we were announcing bad news to the team. We wished the best to those who were leaving, thanked them for their contribution and highlighted their courage in leaving a ship that did not suit them.

From a leadership perspective, this was a great opportunity. By remaining optimistic during a difficult time, Gabriel and I could model the behaviors we wanted to see in the team: positivity, adaptability and resilience. We told the team that we wanted to turn this into an opportunity to improve our expertise and our chances of success. It was also a chance to affirm our DNA and who we were.

At the same time, the team was missing one critical component, a medical resource. Each member of the team was invited to call upon their network. Everyone's involvement in our search created a collective effort and boosted engagement.

A few days later, we welcomed Marie-Michèle to the team as our physiotherapist. As we are neither physiotherapists nor healthcare professionals, Gabriel and I asked very few questions about qualifications. She came highly recommended by someone we trusted, so we assumed she was qualified. It was Marie-Michèle's desire to contribute that stood out in our first conversation. She was exactly who we were looking for. A few months later, during RAAM, Marie-Michèle was a *coup de coeur* for most of the team members. Yes, she fulfilled her role and duties as a physiotherapist; that she did perfectly. But the reason why she was so appreciated by the other members of the team was because of her other qualities: a desire to contribute and a tireless drive. It was everything she did outside of her job description that set her apart. Helping in the kitchen, cleaning, organizing equipment, being present at night in the chase vehicle. Marie-Michèle is quite a bee!

We also welcomed Réjean to the team. Réjean is, in my opinion, the man with the biggest heart in the world. In 2020, Gabriel and I did an Everesting by bike. That is to say, we ascended the same hill over and over again, on a bike, until the total elevation gain of the ascents reached 8,850 meters, the height of Mount Everest. It took us 16 hours to get there. Réjean had promised to come and ride with us for an hour, and he showed up at 5 a.m., at the exact time he had said he would be there. I saw Réjean volunteer for hundreds of hours at a camp for young diabetics. I saw him honor all his promises; I saw him get up at ungodly hours to help others, always with a smile. I knew he was a hard worker and that he was highly reliable. I even felt bad for not having thought of him sooner! He was absolutely perfect for the job. Réjean is a model of integrity and resilience.

Plus, having a child with type 1 diabetes himself, he had the mission tattooed on his heart. I sent him a text message to ask him if he would consider the project. Within seconds, without any hesitation, Réjean, the ultimate bee, said yes. He told me that he had to pinch himself, it was a dream for him to be a part of such an endeavour.

Réjean's commitment from the very first second was unwavering. He wanted to be there, he wanted to give it his all. Réjean taught me several things, one of them being that choosing passionate individuals who have the mission tattooed on their heart is much easier than spending a fortune in trying to make unengaged employees engaged.

You might think that since we had lost two eagles, why replace them with bees? Actually, hiring eagles in the first place was a mistake — my mistake. The project, the mission and our shared goal required a team that was made up of a majority of bees.

OUR OFFICIAL RAAM TEAM

Each year, RAAM organizers issue a unique identification number to each team, a number that will never be reused. We were Team 661 of the 2022 solo cohort. After some role-shuffling, this was our team. We chose to illustrate our organizational chart in a circle. We felt this expressed our culture, our commitment to the mission and our co-dependency.

THE BIG RESHUFFLE

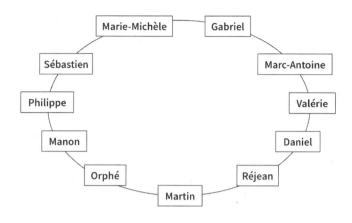

Team 661 of RAAM.

Sébastien Sasseville: Cyclist, project leader
Marie-Michèle Fiset: Physiotherapist and navigator
Philippe Wauthier: Sports director
Réjean Lachance: Driver, responsible for the RV
Orphé Beauchemin: Driver, responsible for all of the vehicles
Manon Gauthier: Cook and diabetes specialist, administration
Valérie Beaudoin-Carle: Social media manager and driver
Gabriel Renaud: Crew chief and navigator
Martin Perreault: Bike mechanic and navigator
Daniel Aponte: Photographer, driver and navigator
Marc-Antoine Legault-Frenette: Videographer

Ready to go! From left to right: Row 1: Gabriel, Philippe, Manon, Orphé.
Row 2: Marie-Michèle, Sébastien, Marc-Antoine. Row 3: Réjean, Valérie, Dan, Martin.

CHAPTER 5

THE BUY-IN

Gabriel Renaud

RAAM is a challenge that took over six months of preparation for just 12 days of racing. While each team member brought with them some very specific professional skills, we also had to invest in "soft skills" and leverage the strengths each individual brought to the table in that regard.

Now, I don't like the term *soft skills* because there's nothing soft about soft skills. It's quite the contrary. I prefer the term *human skills*. At this part in our preparation, we had to get to know each other, create our team alliance and build relationships to foster trust and safety.

LEADING A REMOTE TEAM

Let's set the scene. It's January, and I'm on the phone with Sébastien. He says, "I think we should have team meetings once a month, maybe every two weeks, to plan the project."

My response is not what he expects: "We won't be able to create engagement with meetings at this frequency. We need to meet every week."

Sébastien seems excited by my suggestion. "Yes, I feel the same way, but at the same time, people are busy, and I don't want to overload them. I'm afraid it's asking too much."

I say, "The frequency of the meetings is an important strategy to create engagement. Short but frequent touchpoints are a common trait of every top performing team. If a person can't be there, we'll record the meeting, and they can listen to it offline."

He replies, "Sold, let's go with that!"

Sébastien and I agreed that we wanted no half measures in this team. Engagement often starts with setting the bar high and with a confessed desire of excellence. We wanted people who were fully invested and committed to the mission. We needed this to ensure Sébastien's safety and to successfully cross the finish line before the time limit.

Our team members were scattered throughout the province of Quebec in Canada, mainly in the Quebec City and Montreal areas, which are a three-hour drive apart. This is a reality similar to that of many companies. In addition, due to personal and professional obligations, we were aware that it would be difficult to get everyone physically together more than two or three times before our departure.

In this context, how could we maximize collaboration between team members? How could we ensure the full commitment of everyone despite the distance?

Even with the best preparation, we knew that RAAM would be a challenging beast. It was the resilience of the team, its ability to adapt and collaborate, that would see us through. It was imperative for this group of strangers to get to know each other and build strong bonds, no matter where they were located.

A strategy to foster engagement in remote teams is to have short but frequent meetings.[*] Inspired by this concept, and aware of our reality, we built a five-step plan for creating engagement and a sense of belonging within the team:

1. Individual team onboarding meetings (discussed in chapter 3)

2. Weekly team meetings

3. A team-building day, three months before the race

---

[*] BUCKINGHAM, Marcus, and GOODALL, Ashley. Reinventing Performance Management. *Harvard Business Review*, 2015, vol. 93, no. 4, pp. 40-50.

4. A full-day rehearsal one month before leaving for California

5. Arrival in Oceanside three days before the race

The first goal of the process was to build strong relationships between individuals. Relationships are the foundation of everything. Research has shown that to build a high-performing team, skills alone are not enough. Team members must know each other and share values. Simply put, team members must get to a point where they genuinely care about each other. That's the ultimate goal for leaders in organizations, to facilitate the creation of strong bonds and relationships, even friendships, within their team. The irony is that when the team members are asked to go beyond, for example to come in on a weekend to meet a deadline, they won't do it for the employer. They'll do it for their friends, whom they would never want to let down.

WEEKLY MEETINGS

A culture of continuous improvement is also essential.* By meeting frequently, we would be able to see signs of progress every week. Consequently, the purpose of our weekly meeting was to assess the progress of each pillar of the project and determine the priorities for the following week. The meetings were held online every Wednesday at 7:30 p.m. In a team culture where every minute counts, it was important to be efficient during these meetings. The maximum length of the meeting was set to 45 minutes. We wanted to be respectful of everyone's time while forcing ourselves to prioritize and be efficient. The agenda was prepared in advance by Sébastien and me. Each team member was responsible for reviewing it and adding relevant discussion points based on their area of expertise and responsibility.

These weekly meetings were a central part of our preparation and helped us build momentum as we approached the race. Here is how they were configured:

---

* KAYES, Christopher. *Destructive Goal Pursuit: The Mt. Everest Disaster*. Palgrave Macmillan, 2006.

- Each meeting must be relevant. If it is shorter than the allotted time, there is no obligation to fill the 45 minutes.
- Each meeting must have a clear purpose and objectives so that everyone feels their time is well spent.
- Each meeting must make us more and more accountable.
- Every team member is regularly encouraged to seek help, with dedicated time set aside in each meeting to discuss any obstacles they might be encountering in their current projects.
- We must set aside time in each meeting to celebrate our wins. This is how we establish a culture of recognition within the team.
- Each meeting must be an opportunity to share knowledge. Each member is generous in sharing and does so for the common good of the team.
- Once the weekly meeting is over, everyone is individually responsible for achieving their goals for the week.

Thanks to the constant progress achieved through our weekly meetings, what seemed to be a gigantic mountain to climb now seemed much less daunting. The progress increased our sense of accomplishment and was very motivating. Everyone felt like they were part of something that was producing tangible results and had a significant impact on the mission. If we needed to adapt and change the plan, we did so immediately. The more often and quickly we adapted, the easier it was to correct course.

In the end, although everyone's participation in this venture was voluntary, in the six months leading up to the departure, the attendance rate at the meetings was about 90 percent. In other words, everyone found them of great benefit.

While these team meetings proved to be key to our success, it was critical to balance their frequency to avoid overwhelming the team. Overloading schedules with meetings can lead to hyper-communication, diminishing productivity and giving a misleading sense of effectiveness due to a full calendar. Being busy doesn't necessarily mean being productive.

In order to be effective, the meeting owner must clearly share its objective(s). This allows the invitees to determine if their presence will be relevant to its goals and whether they should participate or not. Therefore, we need to ask: Will each person contribute to achieving the meeting's goals? Who doesn't need to be there? Do I really need to be there to assist? Might it go better without me? This approach ensures that meetings are not just time spent, but time invested wisely.

Soliciting post-meeting feedback is a valuable practice for gauging its effectiveness. This requires courage on the part of the organizer, but also fosters an environment where participants feel safe to share honest feedback without fear of repercussions. Encouraging such an environment, especially through anonymous feedback, allows for immediate insight into the meeting's value to team members and offers guidance for enhancing future meetings.

A share of courage is also required from invitees to decline to attend a meeting, regardless of one's status in the organization. But effectiveness is about learning to say no much more often than yes. And when you feel like you're not wasting your time, you're much more engaged.

THE TEAM-BUILDING DAY

At this point in our preparation, we had already held several virtual meetings, but the team didn't really know each other yet — at least not in person. Our plan was to gather everyone together for a full day of team-building. The purpose of the day was to get to know each other, define our culture and team alliance and continue our logistical preparation.

Being co-founder of the team-building firm Hubu,[*] orchestrating this day was within my wheelhouse, leading to a successful gathering in early April. I was very excited to meet the entire team in person, many for the first time, and to contribute my expertise. In order to make the most of the day myself, I entrusted the facilitation responsibilities to my father, Daniel, co-founder of our firm.

Once everyone was gathered, Sébastien shared a few opening remarks to remind us why this day was happening: "RAAM is a challenge where we will need everyone to be at their best to succeed. To be at our best, we will have to work together, and that's why we are here. To build strong connections."

---

[*] www.hubu.ca/en

When the context is rich in meaning, it helps people understand why it is imperative to make an effort to collaborate. Understanding why we're doing something and why something matters motivates us to commit more deeply to the mission.

Conversely, if we don't understand why we do what we do, how can we fully engage? When people find meaning in what they do, it inspires and motivates them, and as a consequence they become more productive.* This principle applies to all areas of our lives. Our ability to create meaning is directly related to our ability to gather people around an idea. Sébastien is a great example of this.

Knowing how to create meaning is crucial to the process of creating team cohesion. Without meaning, a team-building exercise is merely a treasure hunt or playful activity between colleagues, a nice break or a recess. Without meaning, a team-building activity can be enjoyable, but its impact will be short-lasting.

A team-building process is an opportunity to work on things that will have a real impact on the results and profitability of the business. It is an investment that allows us to foster more engagement, to work better together, to define the culture, to address potentially problematic issues, to express our expectations and to identify our fears.

Sometimes this process can even be challenging, but that's a sign that you're doing it right. Successful team-building can sometimes require humility, honesty, openness and courage to get to know each other. In short, a team-building effort is everything but a recess. Building a team requires deep commitment. It also takes work, time and effort. At times, it means being willing to open ourselves up to exchanges that can make us uncomfortable. At times, it's allowing ourselves to slow down in order to lay the foundations to go even faster.

GETTING TO KNOW EACH OTHER

The first step of the day was an icebreaker activity. We used TeamTalk, a team conversation game that I created with my father, Daniel. The game

---

* GRANT, Adam. *Give and Take: Why Helping Others Drives Our Success*. Penguin, 2013.

generates conversations that allow us to get to know each other better, offer recognition to others and sometimes initiate difficult conversations. We did a round with the first-level cards so that everyone could share something that others didn't know about them.

We learned some important things from this exercise. For example, one question in the game is: what do you do to recharge your batteries? One team member shared that he sometimes likes to take time away from the group to recharge. This information was beneficial to all team members, as during RAAM this individual regularly took time alone for himself. Rather than worrying or bothering him, we knew he was trying to recharge and left him alone in peace. As you get to know your team members, you learn to be more accommodating of each other.

Remember that almost any time can be an opportunity to better understand each other. The context changes, people evolve and experience different things at different times. Therefore, it is important to continue this process, even with a team whose members seem to know each other well.

DEFINING OUR TEAM ALLIANCE

The day was just beginning. Together, we defined our team alliance — a set of rules for how the team wants to work together. The alliance helps the team clarify responsibilities and shows team members how they can support each other most effectively. In our case, how do we want to collaborate during RAAM? How do we want to behave towards each other? What are the non-negotiables that increase our chances of success?

Establishing a team alliance helps the group determine what is and is not allowed within the team. With agreed-upon rules, the potential for conflict is reduced. These rules are often deeply related to the culture and DNA of the organization.

The team alliance is also called the operating rules, collaborative agreement or code of conduct. It is one of the most important aspects of creating psychological safety in the team.[*] The team alliance was crucial for us

---

[*] HAWKINS, Peter, and COYNE, Sue. Creating a Team Alliance for Psychological Safety. Global Team Coaching Institute.

because we were going to live in tight spaces, endure sleep deprivation and be under considerable pressure for more than two weeks. The likelihood of conflict was very high. This agreement was the foundation of our team and the shared experience we wanted to create. Having it on paper was a mutual commitment to hold each other accountable for our actions and behaviors.

After a full team-wide discussion, here are the final elements we decided upon for our collaborative agreement:

- **Respect:** Respect for others and the rules of the race, at all times. Sportsmanship beyond reproach.

- **Tolerance:** Each individual does his or her best. Be tolerant, because mistakes will be made.

- **Structure:** Everything in its place, with a military mindset. Respect the systems and responsibilities of others.

- **No Ego:** Failures and successes are shared. Don't take anything personally. Be able to admit mistakes and ask for help.

- **Performance:** Always provide your best effort.

What happens when this exercise has not been carried out in a team? There is an adage that says, "No agreement, no expectations." Without a clearly defined agreement concerning the various functions each member will fulfill, each individual creates their own expectations. This sometimes becomes a source of disagreement, as there is bound to be a mismatch between the expectations of each individual team member. Team members hope that their colleagues will meet their needs, which, if those needs are not defined, does not always happen.

In our team, expectations surrounding performance were a good example. Sébastien and I had very high standards of performance and excellence, where every detail counts. We knew that, at the end of the day, a few minutes could make the difference between finishing and not finishing RAAM. It was important to accentuate this expectation to the rest of the team and solidify it in an agreement. If everyone accepted this standard of performance, it was expected that all team members would always give their best effort.

The team alliance is an important step in team-building. When individuals agree to such a code, they tend to put their individual interests aside for the common goal. It is also a crucial step in developing the engagement and motivation of each team member. When there is agreement, I am part of something bigger than myself. The team alliance acts as an unseen bond, unifying and guiding our behavior.

OUR TEAM'S CULTURE: A LIGHTHOUSE THAT GUIDES US THROUGH STORMS

The team alliance was the perfect bridge to discuss and define our culture, which allowed us to outline acceptable and unacceptable behaviors within the group. Defining culture is about putting on paper a set of guiding principles for our actions, behaviors and attitudes. Culture is the lighthouse that guides us through storms.

To me, culture resembles an omnipresent observer of our team's dynamics. What would this observer note about us? Would they highlight our unfaltering work ethic, our collaborative spirit or the depth of our expertise? Culture isn't just words you express for show. Rather it's the essence of your day-to-day interactions and actions once you step through the doors of an organization. Culture is lived and embodied in everyday small gestures, in the way people talk to each other and in the way they work.

Even though the team was only three months old, we could already pinpoint words to describe what we were experiencing together. Through all these points of contact, our DNA was beginning to form. The objective of the exercise was to identify three words defining who we were. Then it was to define how each word translated into behavior within the team.

Here is the fruit of the work of this exercise:

- **Performance:** Every minute counts. Every detail counts. Every decision counts. Always commit to your best effort.
- **Collaboration:** Clearly defined roles and an understanding of our interdependence. Each individual clearly communicates his

or her needs and comes to the aid of the others. We are one team with one shared goal.

- **Adaptation:** Always be on the move. Always be agile. Always be solution-oriented. Always be positive.

This was our team culture, and we were proud of it! To bring this culture to life, we decided to produce T-shirts with the words *performance, collaboration* and *adaptation* on the back.

These shirts became our uniform during the race — a tangible reminder to live this culture through every move and decision.

COMMITTING TOGETHER

After a logistical simulation exercise that I will recount in the next chapter, the last activity of the day was to individually formulate and express our commitment to the team. It would be a sort of oath, where everyone pledged in their own way to give their best effort to complete the RAAM.

At Hubu, our mission is to create unforgettable team experiences, and this team won't soon forget what we did next! Before explaining the activity to the team, we always like to create suspense through music playing in the room. For the occasion, we chose African rhythms.

My father, Daniel, spoke up, "I have an arrow in my hands. Do you have any idea what you are going to do with this arrow?" The team members looked at one another in silence. One team member said, "We're going to break it!" Daniel immediately replied, "Yes, you will break it, but how?"

The uncertainty, combined with the exotism of the music created nervousness in everyone. My father added, "Before I tell you how you're going to break it, you're going to write down on a piece of paper your biggest fear in relation to RAAM."

Once everyone had written down their greatest fear, my father offered more details. "You are going to break the arrow ... with your throat." Each individual would have to come to the front of the room, name their fear and then break an arrow with their throat — literally!

Daniel showed the team how it should be done. The tip of the arrow was placed directly on the throat. The other end of the arrow was resting on the wall, so the arrow was horizontal, thanks to a slight pressure from the body. With a sudden movement, my father threw himself forward. Instead of piercing his skin like one would expect, the arrow broke in two.

Although this exercise probably seems dangerous at first glance, I assure you it is safe. Of course, don't try it at home — it requires professional guidance. It's a mental exercise that pushes people out of their comfort zone to the forefront of their limits. It requires total commitment — without that, it can't be done. This was a great analogy for what we would experience during RAAM. To succeed in the mission, it would take absolute commitment from everyone.

To set an example, I was the first to go. I began by naming my fear: "I'm afraid I won't live up to my role as crew chief and team leader." Then I walked over to the wall where I had placed a target and put the plucked end of the arrow on it. In the center of the target, I had written our mission: complete RAAM. I pressed the tip of the arrow against my throat — specifically, the soft spot just above the junction between the sternum and the collarbone. Then, with all my strength, I pressed against the arrow and took a step forward. As the team looked on nervously, the arrow shattered into three pieces.

First steps are hard, but they lead us to something greater. I felt in my heart that the beginning of this adventure was the beginning of something that would have a deep impact on my life.

Sébastien was the second to come forward. He named his fear: "I'm afraid that I won't have the time to adequately prepare as an athlete because of my work commitments." Essentially, Sébastien shared the same fear as me, of not being up to the task.

Each team member took turns in breaking their arrow. Each individual shared their vulnerability by naming their fear, which was an expression of courage. The exercise was a touching and defining moment for our team. Interestingly, expressing vulnerability together rather than alone is much easier, and it nurtured our culture and a collective feeling of psychological safety. We all had fears, but together we could overcome them.

Psychological safety is when everyone feels free to speak up and respectfully communicate their opinions without fear of repercussions. It's about not feeling judged for speaking up, about being able to admit you're wrong and about being at ease asking for help.

Under Philippe's supervision, Sébastien breaks his arrow.

In 2012, Julia Rozovsky, a former Harvard researcher and new analyst in Google's Human Resources department, launched Project Aristotle. The study was to discover what made teams successful at Google. After studying hundreds of teams, the researchers found that what made teams successful was not their members, but rather how they worked together. The research revealed five essential elements necessary for a team to perform well. Psychological safety topped the list as the most important factor in predicting team performance.* Creating this climate of safety was therefore one of our priorities during the six months leading up to the race.

One person's area of weakness is often another person's strength. By being vulnerable, we give others the opportunity to offer us help. When we hold space for fear and vulnerability, as we did during the arrow activity, strong bonds are created. When a group of individuals see that they can conquer their fears together, they become a team.

Getting back to the arrow, it's true that some were more hesitant than others. Even so, everyone rose to the challenge with bravery. I was proud of the team and confirmed my belief that everyone was 100 percent committed. The team was going into RAAM with a warrior attitude!

Sébastien's compelling mission and commitment, combined with the momentum created by our weekly meetings and team-building day,

---

* DUHIGG, Charles. What Google Learned from Its Quest to Build the Perfect Team. *New York Times Magazine*, February 25, 2016.

allowed us to bond, build relationships and take ownership. This commitment then translated into meticulous preparation, which allowed us to become a competitive team in every respect, before and during RAAM. Engagement, without a doubt, was the driving force behind our success.

Asking people to perform is putting the cart before the horse. Performance is a consequence of engagement. By first focusing our efforts on engagement and investing the time and energy it deserved, our team was in a position to generate great results.

CHAPTER 6

MARGINAL GAINS

Gabriel Renaud

Accumulating marginal gains leads to exceptional results. Several authors, such as James Clear, have highlighted this concept. In *Atomic Habits*, Clear recounts how the new sporting director of the British road cycling team, Dave Brailsford, applied the idea. Britain had never won the Tour de France in its 100-year history. In 2003, Brailsford set out to change this by employing this concept: "If you improve all the elements of performance by 1 percent, you will get a significant increase when you put them all together."* Brailsford's idea was to forget about perfection, focus on progression and make micro gains wherever possible.**

The results were outstanding. During Brailsford's reign, the fortunes of British cycling were transformed, with 178 world championships, 68 Olympic gold medals and five Tour de France victories.***

---

* HALL, David, JAMES, Derek, and MARSDEN, Nick. Marginal Gains: Olympic Lessons in High Performance for Organisations. *HR Bulletin: Research and Practice*, 2012, vol. 7, no. 2, pp. 9-13.

** HARRELL, Eben. How 1% Performance Improvements Led to Olympic Gold. *Harvard Business Review* [online]. 30 October 2015. Available from: https://hbr.org/2015/10/how-1-performance-improvements-led-to-olympic-gold.

*** CLEAR, James. *Atomic Habits: An Easy and Proven Way to Build Good Habits and Break Bad Ones*. Avery, 2018.

Exponential Effects of Small Steps

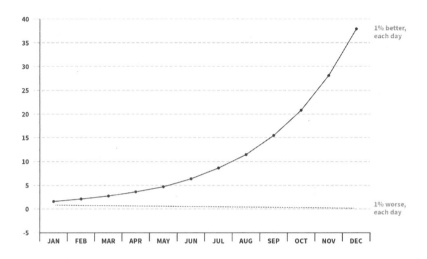

The compounding effects of marginal gains.
One percent better every day can make a big difference.

When Sébastien asked me to join the team, Dave Brailsford's story came back to me. How could we replicate that progression through our preparation for RAAM?

For me, it was through flawless logistics where every detail was planned down to the second. Nothing could be left to chance. Sébastien and the rest of the team agreed. We became obsessed with our logistical preparation. This race is mainly about two things: efficiency and consistency. Making sure that the stops are as short and as optimized as possible, and enabling your athlete to always be moving forward.

Sébastien and I read everything we could about this mythical event. Manon — our cook, diabetes specialist and administrator — and I participated in a two-day webinar offered by RAAM organizers. Sébastien tracked down and invited two participants from previous years to come and share their experience during one of our team meetings.

Each year, the list of participants who successfully complete RAAM is very small. Achieving success demands flawless execution across all aspects of the race, including precise navigation of the course, meticulous management of work shifts, comprehensive strategies for both physical and emotional rejuvenation and, for us, effective management of Sébastien's diabetes.

SUPPORT TEAM SHIFTS

The success of our logistics would be based and depend on the execution of every shift. We had several options for Sébastien's schedule and our support shifts. Some cyclists opt to sleep at night to maintain a semblance of a normal sleep pattern; others prefer to sleep during the day to avoid the incredible heat.

Each team must also determine their vehicle strategy. We chose to have three vehicles for the race: two minivans that we named V1 and V2 and a 30-foot trailer that we named RV. V1 was the chase vehicle that would follow Sébastien at all times.

According to the race rules, from 7 p.m. to 7 a.m., a direct follow rule applies, which means that the chase vehicle must directly follow the cyclist at a distance of no more than 10 meters at all times. Without the chase car, a cyclist is not allowed to ride at night.

From 7 a.m. to 7 p.m., the chase vehicle must operate in "leapfrog support," meaning that it doesn't directly follow the cyclist but rather moves ahead to set up aid stations and the like. Of course, all traffic laws must be obeyed.

V1 was designed to always have three people on board: a driver, a navigator and Philippe, our sports director, who made V1 his home during the race. Philippe had challenged himself to be in the chase car 24/7, throughout the entire race. A small bed was set up so that he or another team member could rest at any time of the day or night.

V2 was our shuttle vehicle to transport team members between shifts. In addition to its shuttle duties, V2 was also the primary vehicle for Dan and Marc-Antoine, our photographer and videographer. By having their own vehicle, they were able to create exceptional content for our social networks and magical memories for the entire team.

The RV was our mobile oasis, the place where Sébastien and the team could rest, where Manon cooked and where all our equipment was stored.

For several weeks, Martin — our bike mechanic and navigator — and I worked out a shift strategy for the team. Each shift involved a change of driver and navigator for V1. To minimize driver and navigator fatigue, we initially decided to run four six-hour shifts. In theory, shorter shifts and frequent crew rotation would allow us to better conserve energy.

FROM THEORY TO PRACTICE

A few weeks before the full-day rehearsal in May, we had completed our strategic and logistical planning. Now we needed to go into the field, test it all out as much as we could and learn from our mistakes. Staying in the "theoretical" stage was beginning to hurt us; we were starting to waste time going into planning minutiae.

Over-planning often happens when people want to avoid making mistakes. Ironically, the best way to make progress is to make mistakes, ideally in a controlled environment. Four weeks before the start, we gathered the whole team for a dress rehearsal: a 200-kilometer ride. We made many mistakes during the practice day, but since we were in a humble and learning state of mind, the day was fun.

We were hoping to see what worked, what didn't and what we'd forgotten. We ran through everything: feeding Sébastien, doing the insulin cartridge change, addressing an emergency situation, practicing the vehicles choreography, going through a crew change in the chase car, and direct-follow night driving. We wanted to test everything, get as much wrong as possible and improve our systems.

While everything seemed to be in place, we had to face the fact that there was a major problem with our shift plan. Doing four short shifts was cutting into our sleep time. We never had a break; we were always on the go. In addition, each shift change greatly increased the risk of navigational errors.

By doing this trial run, we had the opportunity to notice these issues. We immediately changed our plan and decided to adopt a much simpler strategy: a night shift and a day shift.

17:00 to 7:00	Night shift
7:00 to 14:00	Day shift
14:00 to 14:25	Seb to Bed
14:25 to 16:35	Sébastien sleeps
16:35 to 17:00	Seb to Bike

Our daily schedule at RAAM.

The more time spent developing a strategy, the greater the risk that we will become overly attached to it. Sometimes the best course of action is to abandon the original plan and start from scratch. This requires humility and being able to admit that we were wrong. Martin and I had worked for hours on the initial strategy and, frankly, it looked great on paper. In practice, not so much.

WHAT GETS MEASURED GETS IMPROVED

The team gained confidence as preparation progressed. The plan was for Sébastien to be on the bike every day for 21 hours straight. We had to find the most efficient way to get Sébastien from the bike to the bed and from the bed to the bike. These were instances of what we identified as key "performance moments"; we called them Seb to Bed and Seb to Bike.

Peak performance is not about being good all the time, it's about being unbeatable when it matters most. Peak performance is about syncing your best performance with those moments most important to success.

During a performance moment, the entire team's focus and energy must be directed towards flawless execution. For example, to simplify and most efficiently execute the Seb to Bed and the Seb to Bike transitions, all necessary items were meticulously organized within designated storage boxes — maintaining a strict "a place for everything, and everything in its place" policy. Woe to anyone who mixed up or misplaced their contents!

Here are some of the actions that had to be taken for a Seb to Bed. Before Sébastien's arrival:

- Check in, prepare room
- Place nutrition on the table: egg, avocado and liquid proteins with no sugar
- Place resting clothes and personal hygiene accessories in the bathroom
- Set up the physiotherapy table
- Lay out charger and wires for insulin pump, cellphone and watch

When Sébastien arrives:

- Wait for Sébastien at the motel entrance
- Take care of Sébastien's bike right after he dismounts
- Guide Sébastien to the room, where the designated support team is waiting
- Sébastien takes a shower
- Manon administers an insulin injection and manages diabetes care
- Manon weighs Sébastien
- Marie-Michèle conducts physiotherapy
- The team assesses the day's progress

Does the team take the opportunity to rest while Sébastien sleeps? Definitely not! We worked non-stop to prepare for the next day: recharge the batteries of Sébastien's communication and navigation systems, prepare V1, prepare the bikes, conduct vehicle maintenance, prepare the next day's navigation, book the hotels and a dozen other tasks.

As soon as Sébastien woke up, we went into Seb to Bike mode. The goal was to get him back on the bike as quickly as possible. Here are some of the actions that had to take place:

- Ready equipment (before Sébastien is up): clothing, helmet, shoes, glasses and the communication system
- Wake up Sébastien
- Do physiotherapy
- Apply sunscreen and buttocks lotion
- Provide a high-carbohydrate meal
- Help Sébastien get dressed while he eats

Every misstep in our performance moments could make a difference at the finish line. Twelve minutes lost, morning and night, is 24 minutes a day. Over 12 days, that's 288 minutes — almost five hours. And that's without counting all the other minutes so easy to lose here and there. In the end, we estimated that well-done logistics could save us between six and 12 hours. On a race that is won in about 10 days, but with a time limit of 12 days, that's huge!

That's why the efficiency of each Seb to Bed and Seb to Bike was constantly evaluated and measured. Pearson's Law states: "When performance is measured, performance improves. When performance is measured and reported, the rate of improvement accelerates."* The best performing organizations measure the right metrics and, more importantly, implement actions to improve them.

DIABETES MANAGEMENT

Managing Sébastien's diabetes brought its own set of challenges and made our logistics much more complex than those of any other team. Nothing could be left to chance, both to enable him to perform but first and foremost to keep him safe.

Sébastien has type 1 diabetes, the most severe form of the disease. It is an autoimmune disease that has destroyed the beta cells in his pancreas. Type 1 diabetics represent only 10 percent of diabetics. It is a genetic condition and not related to diet and lifestyle. The pancreas no longer produces insulin, the hormone responsible for lowering blood sugar levels. A normal blood sugar level for a non-diabetic is between five and eight mmol/L. This level is naturally regulated by the pancreas. In type 1 diabetics, that function is replaced by insulin injections or an insulin pump. For type 1 diabetics, maintaining blood glucose in range requires constant work and calculations, even when they use an insulin pump and continuous blood glucose monitors.

Throughout the race, our goal was to keep Sébastien's blood sugar between six and nine mmol/L. If his blood sugar gets too low (below

---

* WICK, Doug. Pearson's Law. *Positioning Systems* [online]. 15 December 2008. Available from: https://positioningsystems.com/blog.php?entryID=67.

four mmol/L), Sébastien becomes hypoglycemic. This causes tremors, decreased cognitive and physical abilities, loss of energy, confusion, cold sweats, etc. Hypoglycemia means an immediate forced stop, as he can no longer ride. Hypoglycemia is a serious danger, and quick-acting sugar must be consumed immediately.

If blood glucose levels continue to drop to below three mmol/L, he risks losing consciousness; in extreme cases, death is a possibility.

Conversely, if sugar levels rise too high — above the 10 mmol/L mark — it is called hyperglycemia. This impairs performance but isn't dangerous if it only lasts a few hours. Prolonged hyperglycemia causes dehydration and fatigue and mainly long-term complications. That being said, if untreated for several days, and if insulin levels are insufficient in the body, hyperglycemia can cause ketoacidosis, and death.

Thanks to technology, all team members could see Sébastien's blood sugar levels in real time on their phones. During our dress rehearsal in May, one month before the race, diabetes management was easy — too easy! From start to finish, Sébastien's diabetes was under control. However, there was one thing we missed. Sébastien was fresh as a daisy, not sleep-deprived. He was in full control of his blood sugar management. During RAAM, Sébastien's cognitive state was going to be totally different, and managing his blood sugar was going to become our responsibility. Still, the run-through helped us gain a better understanding of the disease and more confidence in how to manage it.

HESITATION KILLS PERFORMANCE

A few weeks before our simulation, I had the chance to crew Sébastien on a 400-kilometer training ride. My job was to refuel him every 50 kilometers. Deep into the ride, because of his fatigue, Sébastien was slow to answer simple questions like: Do you want me to hold your bike? Do you want to put on some sunscreen? Do you want a brownie or a candy bar? Do you want to change your bib? Do you have enough water left in your bottle? Sébastien's hesitations and reflection time created too many delays. We had to take control of the breaks, eliminate all decisions for him and welcome him with a precise plan of action.

Hesitation is the enemy of the clock. The 10 seconds to make a choice between a brownie or an energy bar. The 10 seconds to decide whether or not to get off his bike. Such moments of hesitation add up and quickly turn to minutes. We didn't have to ask Sébastien if he wanted to change a half-empty water bottle, we just had to do it. Period.

I hold the conviction that making a mistake through action is invariably more forgivable than inaction. Such missteps offer invaluable lessons that propel our growth. This is a philosophy that was important in our team: move forward without hesitation, learn from your actions and continually improve.

RISE ABOVE THE FOREST

Navigation, until a few days before departure, was the elephant in the room. Intuitively, Google Maps seemed like the best option. However, Google Maps always tried to redirect us on the shortest route and only let us enter eight intermediate waypoints between two destinations. Google Maps was therefore not suitable when planning for segments with more than eight turns between time stations. For several months, I worked hard with Martin to find a solution to this problem, but to no avail.

Before the race, the RAAM organization provides teams with a 100-page manual with all the turns to take during the race. Although this manual is useful, it is a secondary tool to a GPS navigation system, which makes it much easier to stay on the course. Racers are obligated to follow the exact route and not miss a turn. Taking a shortcut, voluntarily or not, will likely result in disqualification.

However, the solution, which lay right under my nose, was obvious. In a discussion with Sébastien, he said, "Why don't we use Strava for the car? At the end of the day, you'll be riding at the same speed as me, right behind." Like thousands of cyclists, Sébastien was using this app on his bike. I enthusiastically replied, "This is genius, why didn't I think of it before!"

Have you ever been so close to a solution that it was practically within reach, yet it remained unseen? I was too enmeshed in the details to have a clear view, too close to the trees and unable to see the forest. Sébastien, who was less involved in the navigation issue, was able to rise above the trees, look at the problem with a different perspective and identify the simplest solution.

Sometimes, solving a problem or finding an innovative solution means seeking advice from people who have a different vantage point, a different vision — people from a different industry, for example. Teams composed of individuals with diverse backgrounds and expertise are usually able to find simple solutions to complex problems more easily and quickly than more homogenous groups.[*]

Also, the ability to rise above the forest is a key leadership skill. To achieve this, leaders must first create some space for themselves to "slow down" and take a step back from the sometimes overly narrow focus on operations. In a train or car, you can see the landscape better at 20 km/h than at 120 km/h. It is often hard for high achievers to slow down, but doing so is highly beneficial in the long run and helps to broaden our perspectives.

WHAT WE BECOME

The previous year, when Sébastien cycled across Canada in 16 days, a great heat wave hit western Canada. It was so intense that a "heat dome" formed — a meteorological phenomenon pretty well unknown in Canada until then. While Sébastien was preparing his departure from Vancouver, the mercury reached 50 degrees Celsius in some places. Unlike RAAM, this undertaking was not an organized race, so his departure could have been delayed.

As I was not part of his support team, I was following Sébastien's updates on social media. Sébastien had not promoted it, but he was trying to break the Guinness record for the fastest crossing of Canada by bike.

In my opinion, he should have delayed his departure until the heat wave passed. His chances of breaking the record were nil in that heat. It was unreasonable and even risky to ride a bike in that temperature and humidity — everyone knew it. I even texted Sébastien to ask him if he would consider delaying the start, but his excitement and enthusiasm were

---

[*] POETZ, Marion, and VON HIPPEL, Eric. To Innovate Better, Find Divergent Thinkers. *Harvard Business Review*, 2015, vol. 93, no. 6, pp. 26-28.

too strong. He couldn't wait! And anyway, when you are riding across Canada, you just know the weather is going to be a challenge sooner or later. Perfect conditions do not exist, so he decided to go for it.

Sébastien's toughness and discipline allow him to accomplish seemingly impossible things, even with a medical condition that puts him at a disadvantage. As indicated in the subtitle of the French edition of his first book — "Choosing the Obstacle That Makes Us Grow" — Sébastien consciously chooses to put himself in difficult situations to learn and grow from them.

To Sébastien, the heat dome compounded the challenge and made it even more exciting. It was at this point that I realized one thing about him: he was looking for experiences, not results.

In all of his challenges, Sébastien focused on the process and the mission; the result was one of many components of the overall experience. If he broke a record, great — the story would be even better. But that was not the main objective.

For RAAM, he viewed things the same way. Sébastien never focused on a time goal. His goal was to complete RAAM and for each team member to have an unforgettable experience. This isn't to say that Sébastien, our sports director Philippe and I didn't have expectations in terms of results; of course we wanted to do well.

However, we never made it a priority in our communications to the team. Rather, the priority was for everyone to take ownership of the project, have a positive and enriching experience, understand their responsibilities, and give their best effort every day. Inevitably, the consequence of these best efforts would be a result we could all be proud of.

I understood that Sébastien's recipe for performance was the following: what matters isn't the result but rather what you become. He passed this recipe on to us through our preparation for RAAM. The message to the team was never to make the podium, it was to create a memorable collective experience. By caring about their experience, Sébastien made every team member happy, proud and motivated. And by doing so, Sébastien ensured that he would have a highly committed team to support him and enable him to deliver the best possible performance.

After six months of preparation, it was finally time to fly to California. All of the team, except for Sébastien and Philippe, who had left earlier, boarded the plane in Montreal. Everyone was smiling with excitement and pride. We had worked hard to earn the right to be on the starting line. Together, we were going to live something special, something that we had chosen to experience. We knew we were in the midst of creating memories we'd cherish for the rest of our lives.

During the flight, I looked out the window at the mountains of Colorado and said to Valérie: "Imagine that Sébastien is going to ride through those white peaks, that he is going to bike across the whole country from coast to coast. All this way that we're doing by plane, he'll do by bike!" It was an incredible undertaking, and we were both grateful to be part of it.

The time to shine as a team had come. All that remained was to see if our preparation would survive the monster of a challenge that lay waiting for us.

PART II

GENERATING PERFORMANCE

It's amazing what you can accomplish
if you don't care who gets the credit.

— HARRY TRUMAN,
FORMER U.S. PRESIDENT

CHAPTER 7

GOING BEYOND YOUR ROLE

Sébastien Sasseville

We spent hundreds of hours on our logistical preparation for RAAM, much of which, for understandable reasons, never really received much attention, either in news coverage or on our own social networks. That is the invisible part of success, the hard work that must be done but that no one sees.

For example, when we attempted to make our RV reservation for the race, the two main national RV rental companies were sold out or did not allow a transcontinental one-way rental. They of course typically allow it, but there was a temporary ban on one-way rentals from California to Maryland, especially because of the race. Too many teams wanting to rent RVs, resulting in an unmanageable number of RVs ending up in the same location. Consequently, we were forced to rent an RV close to home, from a private owner. In hindsight, this was a blessing and it turned out to be a more economical option, as it would allow us to bring all our equipment to Oceanside. Bringing the RV 5,000 kilometers from Quebec to California, with the extra $3,000 for gas, was still significantly cheaper than shipping the equipment to California. Plus, renting an RV from California to the finish line would have meant shipping everything back to Quebec, not to mention having to pay for 11 plane tickets to fly everyone home from Maryland.

One of my fondest memories of RAAM was definitely the three-day stay in Oceanside before the race. This is partly because I actually have very few memories of RAAM, due to the extreme fatigue I endured during the race and the fact that all the race days, although hectic, were quite similar in how they unfolded. Everyone on the team agrees that the days spent in Oceanside were special.

Philippe — our sports director — and I flew into Oceanside on June 8 to get a head start on the final preparations. The rest of the team arrived on Saturday, June 11. A Saturday departure made sense for most team members, as it allowed everyone to work their day jobs until Friday and take time off from the following Monday.

Philippe and I wanted to arrive a few days early for several reasons. First, we wanted time; we didn't want to be stressed. I needed to fully switch to an athlete mindset and maximize rest before such a grueling event. We also wanted to be there early, before most of the teams, to be able to manage any unforeseen events as calmly as possible.

As soon as we arrived, Philippe got down to work. His first job was to assemble the bikes and prepare the pursuit vehicle (V1). He had to organize the equipment, tools, nutrition, bike clothes for various weather conditions and many other things.

We rented two minivans in Oceanside for a one-way journey to Annapolis, Maryland. Philippe and I went to pick up the first minivan the morning of June 9. As this was almost a week before the race, one minivan was available. We had planned to take the second one on the 11th so that we'd have two vehicles to pick up our teammates at the Los Angeles airport.

However, that year a total of 220 cyclists started RAAM, either solo or in teams. Dozens of teams who, you guessed it, also rented minivans. Not surprisingly, the rental companies had rented far more vehicles than they actually had available.

After talking with the rental agent, we learned that the number of minivans was going to be very limited on the 11th. And even though we had a reservation, the small print of the contract stipulated that there was no guarantee anything would be available. The agent also shared with us that they had 10 minivan reservations for Saturday. Several teams would also be headed to the rental counter with reservations in hand.

A LITTLE EXTRA EFFORT

Given the minivan shortage, we decided to show up at the rental place very early on June 11. The rental agency — one of the world's largest — opened at 9 a.m. Embracing our team culture and its "whatever it takes" attitude, we chose to show up at 8:30 a.m. We figured that even if only five of the 10 reserved vehicles were available, we should get one. Upon our arrival, we were indeed first in line.

That morning, a second RAAM team showed up at the rental counter at 8:55. As it happened, only one minivan was available. The second team was distraught, but the early bird gets the worm! It was this kind of small extra effort that made the difference in our race in so many occasions.

We wanted to succeed and understood that this depended on having the right attitude. Because those behaviors were embodied every day by our team leaders, the team became acutely aware of our expectations, and of all the little things we had to do to ensure success. All our actions carry meaning, and we are always teaching. Over time, the team had come to embrace this ethic and always strove to go the extra mile.

TAKING OWNERSHIP OF YOUR ROLE

As planned, we were able to pick up the team at the airport on June 11. The three days leading up to the start were filled with some of my proudest moments. Even though the real test was still to come, these moments were a validation that we were on the right track — that Gabriel and I had created something special.

A defining moment was realizing this was no longer my race. I wasn't looking at a group of people supporting me. We had become one team, with one shared goal and purpose. In Oceanside, I saw a group of bees passionately working more than 12 hours a day. The team was autonomous; each bee knew their tasks and collaborated with the other bees to get the job done. The bees were well trained, motivated and highly engaged.

Let's remember that during our first team meetings six months earlier, the mountain to climb seemed immense and the team relied heavily on me to know where to start. The first few meetings were largely devoted to educating the team about the nature of the challenge ahead. What a contrast six months had made. Each team member had taken ownership of their role and was now the master in their kingdom. In fact, they knew more than I did about their respective roles and responsibilities and no longer needed me. They had become the experts (motivating in its own right!) and were now the ones giving me orders.

Sometimes, managers wish that their employees would take more ownership. What I have learned with this journey is that *them* taking more ownership depends a lot more on *us*, leaders. For our troops to take ownership, they must be given the project and the permission to give it their own colors. They need to be trusted and given freedom. Receiving orders is no fun. Being asked to leverage your strengths to bring a team to its goal, that's a lot more motivating.

The point at which each team member takes ownership of their role is a key moment for a leader, a moment that can change everything in one way or another. Three golden rules apply when this scenario occurs: humility, humility and humility.* A leader surrounds himself with challengers, not disciples. When your team starts to execute successfully without you, it's a sign of great leadership. It's a sign that you've created an environment where individuals can grow, develop and coalesce around a common goal. What a tremendous achievement! Be proud, in the same way that you would be proud of your children becoming responsible, wise, independent young adults who no longer need you. This unequivocally shows that you have been an exceptional parent.

On the other hand, the leader who wants to maintain control over decisions and appear to know it all risks sabotaging everything. The leader who seeks to retain control out of ego when a team has built up momentum will slow it down and hurt its performance. Even worse, engagement will be severely compromised and some individuals will abandon ship. We then enter an endless cycle of arrivals and departures. It becomes very difficult to build a strong, stable and clearly defined

---

* REGO, Arménio, OWENS, Bradley, YAM, Kai Chi, *et al.* Leader Humility and Team Performance: Exploring the Mediating Mechanisms of Team PsyCap and Task Allocation Effectiveness. *Journal of Management*, 2019, vol. 45, no. 3, pp. 1009-1033.

culture. It will also be difficult to create a group that shares a strong desire to fulfill the mission.

During these three days in Oceanside, I was touched by the hard work, initiative and dedication that everyone showed. I was so proud of the work Gabriel and I had done, and I was proud of the team. Professionally, everything was perfect. We had gone from strangers, to team, to family.

We had created something truly special, and I don't use the word *family* lightly.

In a family, everyone has a first name. In a business or a corporate team, you have your job, your role and your responsibilities. And in a family, everyone shares the same last name. In the business context, insert the name of your company or your organization here: that's your last name. Everyone in the company is here to support one shared mission with their individual skills. Sadly, as we all want to succeed in our role, this is often forgotten — that we're all here in support of one goal.

US

In many instances, this strong sense of pride made me emotional. I thought to myself, "It's all fine and dandy to talk about the mission, but at the end of the day, these people are here for me." Like many leaders, I had moments when I felt like an impostor. But from the beginning, I had meticulously been choosing the word *us* in all of my communications. I always talked about our race, our project, our mission. We are going to succeed; we are going to stand out. Together we were going to have a profound impact on thousands of people living with type 1 diabetes.

No longer *my* project, RAAM had become a mission — the team's mission. The dream had become shared, as had the desire to succeed. I was now one player amongst 10 other team members, on a great team, with one common goal.

The challenge for many leaders is to cultivate a consistent level of motivation in their team. To cultivate such engagement and motivation, you need to create a culture of empowerment. An autonomous, self-directed and responsible team where each player is comfortable making decisions so that they can do their best work without having to seek approval. If an employee must always ask permission to make an expenditure, to start a project or to take a decision, that employee's engagement will wane.[*]

At the beginning of the project, we assigned roles according to the strengths and interests of each person. At each of our weekly meetings, Gabriel and I insisted that everyone take ownership of their role. We wanted to see proactivity in decision-making and taking action. Our organization and logistics were composed of several major pillars, and we wanted to see them progress from week to week.

Between words and reality, there is always a transition phase, a moment when people have to tame the power given to them. This phase is crucial, because it is at this moment that the appropriation of roles accelerates or comes to a halt. People are testing whether what they've been told is true; they are testing the culture. "I am told that there is no punishment for making a mistake — is that really true? I am told I have autonomy, but will my decisions be questioned or overturned? I am told that my ideas are welcome, but are they considered and implemented?"

People must have the freedom they need to take full ownership of their role. People will quickly stop taking risks and showing initiative if in reality failure is punished or if their ideas are never considered.[**] And then cynicism sets in.

Every company has a credo, a mission or a list of values. It's often posted on the wall near the reception area or in the cafeteria where employees gather. Displaying nice values is the easy part. Coherence between what you say and what actually happens in the organization — well, that's the real challenge.

A manager is also a Chief Repeating Officer. Telling your people once that they have the freedom to make decisions and to take the initiative is not enough. It must be repeated and emphasized often. It needs to be reinforced and embodied throughout the organization. Gabriel and I had repeated many times — in fact, at every meeting — the importance

---

[*] LIN, Jocelyn Tang Phaik, and PING, Nicole Chen Lee. Perceived Job Autonomy and Employee Engagement as Predictors of Organizational Commitment. *Undergraduate Journal of Psychology*, 2016, vol. 29, no. 1, pp. 1-16.

[**] VADEN, Chris. Punishment: Benefits, Risks, and Alternatives in a Business Setting. Thesis, Liberty University, 2004.

owning their projects and running with them. Slowly, we built trust. Each team member realized that they had the freedom they were promised.

I had a general idea of what RAAM was, but it was like any large project — at the beginning you never really know what you're getting into. Often, in taking ownership of their role, team members bring forward knowledge and insight that the team lacks as a whole. Taking ownership of one's role created a sense of purpose and relevance for everyone. For us, the more initiative team members showed, the more freedom it created for them; they became the experts we wanted to listen to, rather than soldiers we told what to do.

People become empowered when they feel that their talents and ideas are essential to the accomplishment of the mission, when they feel they are making a unique contribution to the project.

AN *ALL-IN* LEADER

Gabriel is a model and an inspiration to me. His discipline, intelligence, maturity and professionalism are impressive. He has a wisdom that is light-years beyond what I had at his age, and honestly, beyond that of many people much older than me.

He's also somewhat proper, serious, conservative and never seeks attention. Two days before departure, the team had gathered on the dock for some photos. It was a beautiful setting, with the sunset on the Pacific Ocean as a backdrop. After the photo shoot and a short walk on the beach, the team broke up into smaller groups and most of us headed home. But Gabriel had already left abruptly, claiming he had an errand to run.

As night fell, Gabriel was still missing at the Airbnb. A little unusual, but no big deal. When he arrived, Gabriel had a big surprise in store for us. He had found a barber shop and had them shave our team number, 661, on the side of his head. I couldn't believe it!

This was definitely out of character for him. Gabriel doesn't drink, he is highly disciplined, makes good decisions, is athletic and eats well 365 days a year. Sometimes I wonder if he is a robot. I just couldn't believe it, so much so that the next morning I wondered if I had dreamed it all.

The impact on the team was extraordinary.

Gabriel found an original way to assert his commitment as a team member.

As soon as we arrived in Oceanside, I was no longer playing a leadership role. I was a lot quieter, less involved in the day-to-day and in my head a lot. At this stage, I had become an athlete only. My athlete role was now the most important task to attend to — I focused solely on my body and my final preparations, and made sure that all my needs for the race were met. In our first morning briefing in Oceanside, I communicated to the team that Gabriel was the man in charge. It was important that I said this so that it was clearly understood and not just assumed. When there were difficult decisions to be made, ultimately it was up to Gabriel, the team leader, to decide. And his haircut sent a strong signal to the entire team: "I'm *all in*, are you?"

In a team or organization, if the leader is not fully invested, how can the others be? Obviously, this is not about getting your company logo shaved into the side of your head. Although, if you choose to do so before your next annual meeting, I want to hear from you and know what kind of impact it generated. The team can *feel* when a leader is invested heart and soul. When a leader has a real and deep emotional connection to the mission, when they are willing to do whatever it takes to get the job done, when failure is not an option, others can feel it, and it is contagious.

Gabriel, with a comical gesture, expressed to the team that nothing but everyone's best effort was expected. That this was a relatively short

12-day mission allowing us to set the bar even higher and to demand total and absolute commitment from everyone.

Building and maintaining engagement is no easy task. It took constant effort to maintain the team's motivation throughout our preparation and during the 12 days of the race. Remember, the team was made up of volunteers. There was no monetary reward. This has always been an advantage for me. I can't pay people. Therefore, I am obligated to create a compelling mission and make engagement a top priority. From there, performance always ensues.

The team consisted of passionate people who all had their own personal motives for choosing to be there, and who were under no external obligation to remain. Without a deliberate effort and a strategy, there is a real risk that the team will lose players or that engagement will fade. In our case, I knew too well that without everyone's full commitment, my performance would suffer greatly.

Consciously or not, I also sent the signal that I was all in during my preparation in the months leading up to the event. The 15-hour training sessions don't lie. Neither do the many individual or subgroup meetings we had. For many months, the team saw me pour my soul into my physical preparation and the planning phase. These months were difficult, and my social life certainly suffered. Getting to the starting line is just as hard as the race itself.

But if I hadn't made those sacrifices, what message would I have been sending to the team? If I'm having beers with friends instead of going to bed at eight the night before a big training session, the message to the team is that my personal enjoyment is more important than the race. And if the race isn't that important to the project owner, why should a volunteer give it their all? If Sébastien is 80 percent invested, why should anyone else give 100 percent?

When leaders regularly demonstrate through their actions that they are deeply and fully committed to the mission, it spreads like wildfire. Team members will want to do the same. Excellence breeds excellence. The best way to inspire others to give their best effort is to lead by example and to provide an extraordinary effort yourself. Often, we don't have to say (or ask) anything, as long as we understand everything we do *means* something.

INTERDEPENDENCE

Clearly defined roles and team members who take ownership of them. So far so good, but something is still missing. Doing your job — even doing your job very well — is not enough. The next step is to understand your impact on other team members and on the mission.

We wanted everyone to be the master of their domain, to be an expert in his or her role. That said, to really do your job well you have to understand that you are a cog in a wheel. That there is something happening before and something happening after you act. In a team capable of great performance, teammates understand that they are co-dependent and co-responsible.

Co-dependent is understanding that my success depends on your success. Before becoming an ultra-cyclist, I spent 10 years mountaineering, which ultimately led to a successful ascent of Mount Everest in 2008. If there's one thing you quickly grasp when you're roped together in the death zone, it's that if you don't do everything in your power to make others successful, you won't succeed.

Philippe played a fundamental role in our team's success. He spent 12 days in the chase vehicle. Twelve days! If I was up, he was up, except for a few naps when I was riding strong and everything was under control. He fed me and fixed my bike. He was a favorite within the team, a real rock star. The extent of his knowledge, his unwavering positivity and his inexhaustible energy made V1 a treat to be in. Philippe is a natural leader, and the whole team listened to him. He planned and managed the breaks like real Formula 1 pit stops. Stopwatch in hand, he coached the team to do better every time. Philippe managed the clothing inventory, choosing how I should dress according to the upcoming weather. He was superb at giving assignments to the bees and helping them continually improve. Philippe's success depended on communicating his needs to V2 and the RV team to get what he needed for the next shift. To succeed, he depended on the bees.

Without Manon labeling my meals with the number of carbs in each sandwich, Philippe would not have been able to shine. Without Valérie, who washed my bike clothes in a plastic bucket, Philippe would not have been able to give me clean, dry and warm clothes.

Co-responsibility means understanding that regardless of one's role or status, we are collectively responsible for accomplishing the mission.

Gabriel and I talk a lot about the importance of having clearly defined roles. When we are co-responsible, teammates know that it is imperative to do more than what's in their job description. Marie-Michèle, our physiotherapist and navigator, was a shining example of this attitude. She was everywhere, helping everyone; she picked the night shifts in the chase vehicle, she helped with cooking, cleaning and much more even though that was not in her job description. The reality is that there were only a few available minutes every day to do physiotherapy. I initially wondered if Marie-Michèle would get bored, but it was very much otherwise!

Co-responsibility is the best way to get rid of the "it's not my job" syndrome and "falling through the cracks" issue. It's about going the extra mile, making the extra phone call, sending the extra email, calling someone to ensure a warm transfer to make sure nothing falls in between two chairs. When you have a co-responsible teammate like Marie-Michèle who is continuously going above and beyond, it inspires others to surpass themselves. With her actions, with her generous and positive attitude, and without any spoken words, Marie-Michèle raised the standards and performance of the entire team.

A SHARED STATE OF MIND

A shared goal is essential to a team's success. That shared goal becomes a state of mind for the team and defines its spirit. Easy to say, but not so easy to create. We had recruited bees, hardworking bees. Our values were collaboration, performance and adaptation. We had spent months gathering the team around a mission.

In just a few hours, the race would begin. Every move, every action was going to have to be consistent with the culture we had created.

As an athlete, I have a competitive spirit. I spent a year visualizing the race on my bike. Beyond the cause and the mission, I wanted to perform, I wanted to fight, I wanted to achieve the best possible performance and surpass my limits.

I arrived on the starting line ready, physically and psychologically, with a warrior's attitude.

CHAPTER 8

NO ONE WINS ALONE

Gabriel Renaud

As we approached the starting line, the sense of nervous excitement was palpable. But beyond that, I also felt Sébastien's sense of pride in finally getting there with his new family. A few minutes before leaving for the starting line, Sébastien came to see me. In a moment of emotion, he said to me, "Thank you for everything you've done, I'm so grateful." To tell you the truth, he could hardly hold back his tears. It was at that moment I realized the impact my involvement had had on him. Throughout the project, Sébastien repeatedly expressed gratitude to everyone on the team. He made it a top priority. With only a few hours to go, it was more proof that, for him, nothing was possible without everyone's contribution. Even the best athlete in the world could not finish this race alone. In life, in sports and in business, no one wins alone.

Receiving this mark of recognition felt great. My partner showed complete trust in me before stepping into the arena. By giving and receiving recognition, we are also fulfilling our own needs for belonging, competence and autonomy, so in the end everyone wins.* It means, "I'm behind you no matter what happens. I'm going to follow you in all your decisions."

---

* DUBREUIL, Philippe, FOREST, Jacques, and COURCY, François. Our Strengths and Those of Others: How to Optimize Their Use at Work? *Gestion*, 2012, vol. 37, no. 1, pp. 63-73.

It was now time to say goodbye to the comfort of our villa. A new adventure on the road was beginning. The entire team climbed into the minivans and headed to the starting line, next to the beach in downtown Oceanside. Since parking is limited in that area, the RAAM organizers requested that teams park their vehicles in lots about 500 meters away.

For safety reasons and to minimize the pack effect, each cyclist starts in turn at one-minute intervals. The first eight kilometers are on a bike path and overtaking is not allowed. Sébastien's departure was scheduled for 1 p.m. sharp. At 11 a.m., we parked our two minivans. Sébastien sat in one of the vehicles to do a short visualization in the comfort of the air-conditioning.

DOES IT SERVE THE MISSION OR MY EGO?

The book *Leaders Eat Last* by Simon Sinek illustrates what I experienced during the next few hours.* It was now 11:30 a.m., and the team was ready to go to the starting line. However, there was an issue. The spare bike on the roof of V1 was not locked, and we didn't have room to store it in the minivans. We couldn't help but admit that someone had to stay behind to guard it. Not the coolest job, but imagine our spare bike getting stolen right at the start!

In the end, as we huddled to raise this concern, I volunteered to stay back and watch our equipment. A few moments later, the team gathered at the start line to cheer Sébastien on, while I found myself alone in a parking lot with the spare bike. Not quite the experience I had envisioned for the start!

Being a leader is always about doing the right thing for the mission. To be frank, what did my ego want at this moment? To be at the starting line with my friends and live this special moment. I sure felt like I deserved to be there. However, the mission demanded something else: someone to guard the bike. Sometimes serving the mission means

---

* SINEK, Simon. *Leaders Eat Last: Why Some Teams Pull Together and Others Don't*. Portfolio/Penguin, 2017.

putting your personal interests second. On the verge of a decision, one question to ask yourself is: "Is this serving my ego or the mission?" Watching the bike was about doing what was needed for the mission. It certainly wasn't for my ego. It was also about embodying the behaviors we wanted to see during the race: no ego and relentless pursuit of the team's interest before one's own.

Philippe also embodied this leadership principle on many occasions. In V1, he always made sure his colleagues had everything they needed to do a great job as drivers and navigators. He always wanted people to sleep before he did, even though he slept far less than the rest of the team. Leaders like Philippe genuinely care about the mission first, understanding that it sometimes requires a sacrifice of their own interests.

MAKE THE BEST OF IT

Watching the bike at Oceanside was something I will always remember. Moments after the team left, a man in his seventies came and stood next to me. I soon learned that he was also watching a team's bike a little farther down the parking lot. He was a retiree crewing for a Swiss cyclist also in the solo category.

My meeting with this man led to a long conversation about life. It was a spontaneous moment that allowed me to understand the motivations of a man his age to be part of a RAAM team. By being curious, I discovered his life journey as well as all the wisdom he had to offer. Later in the trip, I stumbled into this man on three occasions. This was special, as the odds were quite low given the vast territory we covered. It was as if life had put him in my path. Unfortunately, I found out that his team's cyclist dropped out two-thirds into the race due to acute neck pain.

This episode reminded me of the importance of making the best out of every situation, no matter the circumstances. In life, we're often presented with a fundamental choice: to be a creator or be a victim. The Karpman Drama Triangle, a concept from psychology, illustrates this principle. It teaches us that a creator takes full responsibility for their actions and outcomes, always seeking to make the best out of the situation. On the other hand, a victim tends to shirk responsibility, casting blame on external factors or others for their predicaments, and often feeling helpless about changing their circumstances.*

FROM THE OCEAN TO THE DESERT

And just like that, the racers were off. Sébastien was embarking on the toughest ultra-cycling race in the world with no guarantee that he would succeed. The team was also heading into the unknown. Back at the parking lot, everyone got into their respective vehicles, and off we went.

Sébastien on the starting line.

Step number one was to navigate the 142 kilometers to our first time station: Borrego Springs, California. This location marked our first crew change. Sébastien's anticipated time of arrival was 6:30 p.m. The first hours led us across the diverse landscapes of California, from the refreshing

---

* MCMAHON, Dick. The Drama Triangle. *The Skilled Facilitator Fieldbook*, Jossey-Bass, 2005, p. 421.

breezes of the Pacific Coast through the rugged mountain ranges and into the intense heat of the desert.

The race featured over 30 solo teams, each supported by two or three vehicles. To prevent crowding on the roads used by the cyclists and their support teams, the RAAM organizers directed all non-chase vehicles to take an alternate path. This detour led us through challenging mountainous terrain, with deep valleys stretching several hundred meters below. Our head driver Orphé's skillful handling of the 30-foot RV along these windy roads was truly commendable.

With the heat and the repeated braking, we began to smell something burning. Orphé told the rest of us: "Our brakes are getting hot; I'm going to have to stop." Just a few hours into the race, and we were already facing our first technical difficulty. This unexpected halt gave us a chance to capture the scenic beauty reminiscent of the animated landscapes from the Road Runner and Coyote cartoons I cherished in my youth. Luckily, we were nearing the end of the descent, with the route to Borrego Springs promising a much flatter terrain ahead.

Upon reaching Borrego Springs an hour later, I was amazed by the sudden resurgence of greenery in this desert oasis, complete with palm trees and even a golf course.

BUNKING EARLY

Once we arrived at our meeting point in Borrego Springs, we stopped the RV to prepare for the first crew change. Even at 6 p.m., the temperature soared to 42 degrees Celsius, and the sun's rays remained intense, necessitating an additional layer of sunscreen.

As soon as the RV was stopped, Manon got to work preparing lunch and Sébastien's nutrition for the night shift. She meticulously labeled each wrap with its carbohydrate content to ease Philippe's task. With Sébastien's arrival imminent, Valérie and Marie-Michèle lent their support in the kitchen.

Using my phone, I pinpointed Sébastien's location. Marie-Michèle and I were the driver/navigator duo for the first night shift. We awaited V1's arrival, backpacks slung and lunch boxes in hand, reminiscent of school children waiting for their bus. Suddenly, I saw Sébastien in the distance.

Marie-Michèle cheered him on energetically: "Go, Seb, go!" I then remarked to Marie-Michèle, "V1 shouldn't be too long. They must have gone to put gas in."

In line with our strategy, the V1 team was tasked with ensuring their vehicle was fueled before the evening shift to avoid leaving the incoming team with an empty tank. If the chase vehicle stops, the cyclist must also stop. We aimed to avoid that at night, especially for refueling, which could be handled during daylight without interrupting Sébastien.

A few minutes later, I saw V1 approaching. The shift change was quick, and all information was passed on efficiently. Marie-Michèle and I began a 12-hour night shift.

With V1 driving side by side with Sébastien, Philippe asked about his condition: "How are you doing, Seb?" Sébastien glanced at us with a pitiful look and said, "Not too well; I don't have any energy, I'm going to bunk much sooner than I thought." Then, right after that, he gave us a big smile, as if to alleviate our worries.

Merely six hours into the race, Sébastien's vitality seemed diminished. This may be normal for some, but keep in mind, Sébastien is someone who is usually fresh after a 15-hour ride. That's when I realized that the RAAM was not a performance race, but rather a grueling endurance test. Who can withstand the heat and sleep deprivation the longest? Who can eat the most miles and repeat it every day?

The good news was that Sébastien's spirits and energy saw a resurgence a few hours later. He had switched to a much more aggressive and less comfortable bike to ride in the mountains. In Borrego Springs, he asked for a change of bike, and the energy returned immediately. He had just gone through a first round of darkness. In the end, nothing overly abnormal, but we were all learning to dance with the ups and downs of this daunting race.

A FORMULA 1 PIT STOP

The first night went relatively well except for a puncture that forced us to change a tire. The highlight of the first night was Sébastien's first "long" stop — a 10-minute planned stop when he goes to the bathroom, showers, changes his clothes, gets a massage and eats.

A camera crew for a TV show was following us on the first day, so we wanted this stop to be perfect. We aimed for precision in every action. At around 11 p.m., we started making a list of all the things that needed to be done during this stop, which was scheduled for around 12:30 a.m., about halfway through the night shift.

Once we had a list of tasks, we allocated responsibilities based on our respective strengths. Beyond the stop's primary goals, we also needed to ensure the replacement or charging of all bike systems, including the front and rear lights and GPS and communication devices. Philippe, Marie-Michèle and I collaborated seamlessly, aiming for utmost efficiency and coordination in our tasks. We only had 10 minutes to accomplish a lot.

Have you ever witnessed the efficiency of a Formula 1 team during a pit stop? This epitome of teamwork illustrates that performance isn't solely achieved on the racetrack but also significantly depends on the support crew's effectiveness. In such a pit stop, a dozen mechanics are dedicated solely to tire changes: "Four mechanics simultaneously unscrew the tires, four more remove them, four more place the new tires and the first four screw them on with a gun. In case of a breakdown, a second gun is placed at their feet."* We approached all our stops with the same mentality.

One moment I'll remember for a long time was when Sébastien got naked to shower and go to the toilet while the TV crew was filming. Necessity trumped privacy, and the film crew had a front-row seat to the entire process. In the midst of the action, Sébastien was putting on his clean shirt. At the same time, Philippe and the TV show host were shoveling food down his throat and Marie-Michèle was putting on his bike shoes. Quite the scene!

People following our story on social media were only seeing the tip of the iceberg of all that we went through. They were seeing footage of Sébastien pedaling and getting treats like ice cream cones and candy bars. Images of brownies thrown at him out the window of V1 to make sure he

---

* PELTIER, Raphaëlle. F1: The Pit Stop, Secrets of a Handful of Crucial Seconds. *La Presse* [online]. 2 August 2019. Available from: https://www.lapresse.ca/auto/course-automobile/2019-08-02/f1-l-arret-aux-stands-secrets-d-une-poignee-de-secondes-cruciales.

had enough calories while cycling. The TV crew had just witnessed the other side of things, the harsh reality that most people didn't know about. To motivate and inform the team of the progress of the stop, Philippe shouted loudly the number of elapsed minutes. This pit stop was anything but quiet!

In 10 minutes flat, Sébastien was back on the road. He yelled into the microphone, "Whoooohoooo!" Philippe asked him, "What's the matter, Seb?" Sébastien immediately replied, "That was so thrilling and energizing, I want the same thing every night!" It was a moment of great intensity.

The first Seb to Bed was scheduled 550 kilometers from the start in Salome, Arizona, a tiny town in the middle of the desert. Around 7 a.m., the day crew came to replace Marie-Michèle and me. At the shift change point, there were about 75 kilometers to go before we reached our first motel.

When we booked accommodations, we always made sure to have an early check-in and two rooms — one for Sébastien and one for the team. This strategy allowed the team that had just finished the night shift to go immediately to the motel to shower and rest before Sébastien arrived for Seb to Bed.

Around 8 a.m., we arrived at Sheffler's Motel in Salome. The motel was showing no vacancy. This motel was a tactical choice for a stopover for many teams, given the distance covered since the starting line and its isolation with no other accommodations within a 75-kilometer radius. We had planned ahead by booking the rooms in April. We knew very well that this would be the first stop for several teams, and we did not want to be forced to sleep in the RV in the heat.

The motel's owner greeted us with open arms, his demeanor both welcoming and playful. He lightheartedly remarked that we had arrived during Arizona's peak summer heat, joking that we were lucky to have the heat today for the race.

Around 10 a.m., Sébastien and Vi arrived at the motel for the first Seb to Bed. At this point, Sébastien was in 14th place. A Seb to Bed was always a key moment for us, having to get him from the bike to the bed as quickly as possible. Everything went smoothly during this first critical moment and Sébastien went to bed around 10:30 with plans to be back on the road at 1:30 p.m.

DARE TO CHALLENGE DIRECTLY

The heat was stifling outside. Riding in this temperature is flirting with the potentially catastrophic risks of dehydration and heat stroke. At the very least, it puts at risk the performance of the days to come. Philippe came to talk to me: "What do you think about extending Sébastien's sleep?" I answered, "I think it's an excellent decision considering the heat." We decided to extend the first night in the desert from three to five hours. Instead of returning to the road at 1:30 p.m., Sébastien would start pedaling again at 3:30 p.m.

The decision wasn't unanimous. Marie-Michèle, Manon and Valérie voted against it. We were curious to understand their point of view. Marie-Michèle pointed out that "we are in a race, every minute counts and the hours lost early in the race will be difficult to make up later when Sébastien slows." Philippe and I agreed, but countered that we didn't see this time as time lost; rather, it was an investment. Sleeping two extra hours now would allow Sébastien to leave fresher and avoid two hours of cycling at 45 degrees Celsius, which could be very costly later on.

Resistance sometimes shown by teammates is healthy for any team's success. We wanted our teammates to challenge our decisions. This is what author Kim Scott calls "challenge directly" in her book *Radical Candor*. In a successful team, there needs to be a balance of *care* and *challenge*.

Caring, according to Scott, is showing empathy and being able to put yourself in the other person's shoes. It's about wanting to contribute and always having positive intentions in all your communications. To challenge is being able to offer feedback and to question openly.[*]

What happens in a team when one of the two ingredients is missing? An excess of caring without adequate challenge might lead to just saying what people want to hear or even perceptions of favoritism. On the flip side, an overemphasis on challenge without sufficient caring can lead to a hostile environment marked by counterproductive aggression among team members. Achieving a balanced approach between caring and challenge is crucial for a healthy team dynamic.

---

[*] SCOTT, Kim. *Radical Candor: Be a Kick-Ass Boss Without Losing Your Humanity*. St. Martin's Press, 2019.

This difference of opinion from day one showed one thing: psychological safety was well established in the team. The fact that team members questioned our decision demonstrated that they felt confident to communicate openly.

In such scenarios, it's crucial for co-leaders to support each other's decisions. After considering the team's feedback, Philippe and I decided to adjust our original plan, reducing Sébastien's additional rest by 30 minutes. Consequently, Sébastien's departure was rescheduled to 3 p.m. instead of 3:30 p.m.

This situation reminded me of a concept called co-active leadership, applicable when two co-leaders are called upon to collaborate and make decisions together. If one leader chooses a direction, the other aligns with that choice. Co-active leadership acknowledges the potential negative impact on team dynamics and morale that can arise from visible discord or disagreement between co-leaders. This model emphasizes the significance of presenting a unified front to foster a cohesive and motivated team environment.[*]

Philippe and I made a decision with the information we had at the time. Was it the right one? Probably not. Sébastien tossed and turned in his bed and slept for only one hour during the five hours he was in Salome.

When he woke up, Sébastien had dropped nearly 10 positions in the rankings and was now in 22nd place. There was a lot of ground to make up to join the leading pack. Even worse, since he had not been able to sleep, Sébastien's physical condition was far from what we expected to start day 2.

However, Sébastien's sleep was not something we could control. So how could we blame ourselves for our decision-making? Would the outcome have been different if Sébastien had had four hours of restful sleep? Of course it would. And what would have happened if we had left at 1:30 p.m. as planned, if Sébastien had ridden an extra two hours in 45 degrees Celsius? Would he have had a heat stroke? No one knows. Speculation clouds the mind. What's done is done. It wasn't until after

---

[*] KIMSEY-HOUSE, Karen, and KIMSEY-HOUSE, Henry. *Co-Active Leadership: Five Ways to Lead.* Berrett-Koehler, 2021.

the race that we realized the five-hour stop wasn't a good idea — podium cyclists usually ride for 30 to 40 hours before taking their first break.

In the heat of the moment, we kept looking ahead. The bees still had a lot to do!

CHAPTER 9

1 + 1 = 11

Gabriel Renaud

Day 2 was in the desert, and it was full of ups and downs. The second evening shift happens to be one of my fondest memories of RAAM. We were going through the Yarnell Grade climb, a hill several kilometers long overlooking a desert valley. I was on my first shift with my partner, Valérie, and the scenery was otherworldly. The cherry on top of the sundae: we were treated to a breathtaking sunset.

But the Yarnell Grade climb probably doesn't bring back such happy memories for Sébastien. It's a 12-kilometer climb at about a 5 percent grade, but it starts with kilometers of false-flat uphill climbing. Sébastien told us through the communication system: "I think my brake is rubbing on my wheel." We had this problem on the first day, and Sébastien thought it was happening again.

Philippe asked him to pull over to the side. In a few seconds, Philippe quickly checked the wheel and immediately said: "Everything is fine. Your brake is not rubbing on your wheel, the resistance is normal. We are on a false flat." Sébastien replied "Are you sure about that? I think it's going downhill!" Sébastien's cognitive state was slowly deteriorating.

Further up the climb, Sébastien stopped smiling for the first time. To help him through this rough spot, we amicably teased him through the microphone. Nevertheless, Sébastien was suffering through the last kilometers. I got out of the chase car and ran alongside him to keep him company and to cheer him up while he slowly made his way to the top of the climb.

Arriving at the top, Sébastien couldn't take it anymore. He stopped, put his feet on the ground and rested on his aero bars. Philippe — the excellent coach that he is — came over to cheer him up while I gave him a shoulder massage. Sébastien asked us for a cola and some snacks before leaving. This was his darkest moment so far. It was also the first time he had made an unplanned stop of his own free will. We reassured him that everything was fine and that the next 100 kilometers were downhill.

This short nutrition break ended up being very beneficial for Sébastien, who then rode like a maniac through the second night. He caught up with nearly a dozen cyclists that night and completed 414 kilometers on day 2 despite the 6,100 meters (more than 20,000 feet) of elevation gain, which in that respect was the most demanding day of RAAM.

Sébastien was back in 14th position.

THE SHOWER ROUTINE

The morning brought more magnificent scenery. Little by little, the sun rose through the valleys and the cacti. The thermometer also climbed very quickly. By 10 a.m., it was already 38 degrees Celsius. We stopped for gas and, in the distance, I could see the hot air waves above the asphalt. After a few minutes of gassing up, I already wanted to return to the comfort of the air conditioning. I can't imagine what it felt like for Sébastien pedaling in this heat.

If Sébastien's body temperature were to rise too quickly, there would be a risk of dehydration, or worse, heat stroke. In a race like RAAM, such a scenario is catastrophic. The consequences could be as serious as a 12-hour stay in hospital, which automatically would be a withdrawal from the race. To keep our athlete cool, we had planned for two methods.

The first method was a cooling vest. A special vest is filled with ice and is fitted tightly for maximum body contact to reduce the body temperature. However, the vest has its limitations. If the vest is not refreshed regularly, it can become counterproductive, as the ice melts and becomes a mass of warm water. Imagine wearing a 10-pound warm jacket in 45 degrees Celsius.

The second method was to give Sébastien ice showers every 15 minutes, ideally without stopping him. We had a portable "pump shower" with us — essentially, a tank with a hose. To get the water out, we had to pump the tank manually to pressurize it. In the end, this was the technique that worked best.

When we were giving Sébastien the shower from the vehicle, the driver had to drive as close as possible. Then, Philippe, on the passenger side, would spray him with the portable shower hose. When the team was on foot, Sébastien would slow down to less than 10 km/h to allow two team members to run alongside and spray him. One person would hold the tank while another cooled him with the hose. The shower routine was more complicated than it looked! We had to apply the right pressure, run at the right speed, release the pressure and aim well at the right time so as not to miss. It was an art.

Given its crucial importance, this routine became a key performance moment, and the trio of Martin, Réjean and Philippe proved to be the team *par excellence* for this task. Once they had refined their technique, they executed the maneuver with contagious enthusiasm and pride. This was yet again another embodiment of our culture of collaboration and excellence, even in the smallest details.

The duo of Martin and Réjean are about to shower Sébastien with cold water.

DO THE BEST WITH WHAT YOU HAVE

Day 2 certainly had a big surprise in store for us: the RAAM organization announced a route change that forced us to alter the plan on the spot. There were forest fires near Flagstaff, Arizona, which was part of the route. The organizers made us take a new route that would pass through the Hopi Reservation Indigenous community. Gas stations would be very limited in this area, and the motels non-existent, for more than 200 kilometers.

Having worked the night shift in V1 on day 1, I was now in the RV with a crew of four. We arrived in Winslow, Arizona, the last town before the next community, at around 10 a.m. At this point, we had two choices: stop in Winslow and get Sébastien to sleep or continue and get as far along as possible. After a five-hour stop the day before, the choice was obvious: we had to continue and cover more distance. The night allowed us to solidify our place in the ranking, and a stop so early would negate all these gains. However, the town of Tuba City, where I had booked the next hotel, was still 200 kilometers away. By my calculations, we wouldn't be there until 6 or 7 p.m.

The heat slowed down Sébastien, and his condition worsened as the sun strengthened. With the original route, other hotel options were possible, but on this new route, there was nothing. The more the day progressed, the more it became obvious that we would have to find an alternative to Tuba City. We were in the middle of the desert, and I was starting to seriously think about having Sébastien sleep in the RV. However, this option was far from optimal, since the air conditioning was defective.

It was 1 p.m. Using the satellite phone, I contacted Philippe in V1: "How's Sébastien? Can he keep going and sleep in Tuba City as planned?" Philippe answered me right away: "No, change of plan. We are not going to the hotel anymore. Sébastien is completely fried; we have to stop as soon as possible. You need to find an oasis for the RV within 30 kilometers." I replied, "Roger, we'll take care of that!" So, after all, despite the failing air conditioning, Sébastien would have to sleep in the RV. That was the only option available.

Soon, the V2 team would join us to help create a pop up oasis for Sébastien's next stop. The next village was about 20 kilometers from

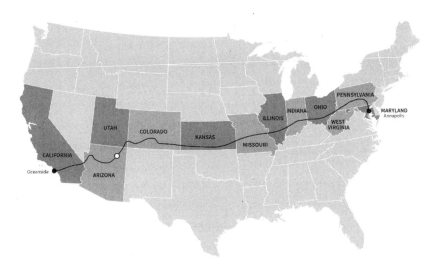

The white dot identifies Second Mesa. With a population of 1,800, it has a convenience store, a small restaurant, a school and a few residential areas.

Sébastien's position, which gave us less than an hour to set up camp. The village was Second Mesa and seemed perfect for an impromptu rest stop.

Arriving in the village, we found a spot behind the convenience store to park the RV. A Seb to Bed in the RV is more complex than in the hotel. The whole team must put its activities on pause and vacate the vehicle to let Sébastien sleep in peace. Not only do we have to gather everything that is needed for Sébastien, but also all the equipment the team will need for the next few hours. We started to set up a temporary camp for the team not far from the RV: outdoor tent, tables, folding chairs, coolers, etc.

PREPARING FOR THE ARRIVAL OF THE QUEEN BEE

Orphé kept the RV engine running with the driver's cabin air conditioning — the only air conditioning that worked — on maximum. We wanted to cool down the whole RV, but that turned out to be impossible with the team constantly going in and out to get organized. Nonetheless, and despite all the unforeseen events of this second day, the bees mobilized themselves to fulfill the most important task at this moment: to prepare for Seb to Bed. We knew that the situation was not ideal, but we had to do the best we could. We had less than 30 minutes before we rolled out the red carpet for the arrival of the queen bee!

The beauty of having a team of 11 people with complementary strengths is the ability to add and even multiply our skills. Faced with a suboptimal situation, our photographer Dan's capacity for thinking creatively kicked in: "I could go to the elementary school and ask them to put us up for a few hours." The school was about 100 yards across the street. I had my doubts and hesitated for a moment. This was a very underprivileged area, which in my mind made the idea even more far-fetched. My expectations were low. Knocking on the door of an elementary school to ask to host a cyclist is not something I would have advocated for.

But I then remembered that one of Dan's areas of genius is Wonder, the ability to imagine different possibilities and think inventively. It's no coincidence that he is such an amazing photographer! For me, Wonder is a zone of frustration. I then realized that in this situation, I needed to step back and let Dan take the lead. I replied, "Good idea. It's worth a shot."

Dan left on his mission. At the same time, a gust of wind suddenly blew down our tent, as if the universe was sending us a message: your current plan is doomed to fail. We recovered the tent, but unfortunately it was destroyed. I now hoped with all my heart that Dan's plan would work, because there was no shady place to take refuge for the next few hours. In the desert sun, we would surely cook.

A few minutes later, Dan returned with good news: "The elementary school will be hosting us for a few hours. They even have air conditioning and showers!" He flashed a smile of pride and satisfaction. The whole team jumped for joy. I was surprised, but relieved.

The strength of a team is to have different types of profiles: introverted and extroverted, creative and analytical, tactical and strategic. This goes with the Confucian concept that, when it comes to teamwork, the whole is greater than the sum of its parts. This is the guiding idea of this chapter — 1 + 1 = 11. By combining different genius types in a team, the weaknesses of one are countered by the strengths of the other and, together, the team can overcome challenges and achieve exceptional results.

A team is not just a group of people who share tasks. A team is a group in which each individual can shine by using their strengths every day.* Compounding strengths is the recipe for success of the most high-performing teams.**

Unsurprisingly, when a team member is having difficulty giving up their place to let a colleague shine, it will have a negative impact on the team's performance. The message sent by the person not wanting to give up their place is that, for selfish reasons, they are holding the team back. The team member who is deprived of the opportunity to shine will feel like their expertise is not being recognized. This can quickly lead to the disengagement of that individual.

It is by contributing with our individual strengths that we can succeed collectively. Humility is therefore a crucial quality, because in successful teams, the success of the mission always takes precedence over the personal interests of individuals. In our case, we were all ready to let each other shine.

We only had a few minutes before Sébastien arrived. We had to settle quickly in the school. Like a beehive, the purpose of the school was to host our "queen" and to provide security to the colony, a shelter against bad weather. Like little bees at work, we transported all the necessary accessories from the RV to the school gym.

As usual, even though he was suffering, Sébastien arrived with a big smile. He seemed very happy to see that he would spend the next few hours in cooler temperatures and that he would be able to take a real shower. The team jumped into the Seb to Bed routine with great efficiency. We accomplished the mission to put our queen to bed in relative comfort.

RELIABILITY = PERFORMANCE

The work was far from over. The period when Sébastien slept was always busy, as we had to prepare for his awakening and the departure that followed.

---

* RATH, Tom, CONCHIE, Barry, *et al. Strengths Based Leadership: Great Leaders, Teams, and Why People Follow.* Simon and Schuster, 2008.

** BUCKINGHAM, Marcus. *Go Put Your Strengths to Work: 6 Powerful Steps to Achieve Outstanding Performance.* Simon and Schuster, 2007.

This is especially true for Manon, our cook, who would take control of the RV for those few hours. As we approached the RV, we could smell the chicken cooking inside. The energy of the team was high, thanks in large part to the healthy and varied meals prepared for us every day. Manon played a big role in maintaining the team's vitality. One of Manon's geniuses is Enablement, and it showed. Manon always wanted to help others, and she easily adapted to any situation to help get us where we needed to go.

Manon wasn't the only member of the team who worked hard to prepare for Sébastien's wake-up call. On the to-do list was the reloading of the vehicles for the next day. Réjean was often the one who filled up the coolers and made sure there was enough ice and water. We also had to maintain Sébastien's bike and prepare his clothes. Martin is an avid cyclist and was responsible for the mechanics. Orphé oversaw the vehicles. He ensured that the gas tanks were full and that everything else in the vehicles was in order.

We were also fortunate to have a media team to chronicle our race. Valérie, Dan and Marc-Antoine worked tirelessly to prepare the next video or photo for social media. From shooting to editing to sharing files to posting on social media and sharing content with our PR firm, they not only collaborated brilliantly but also created a whole production chain. I know for a fact that they went above and beyond what Sébastien had asked of them. Sébastien simply had chosen the right players, shared a clear vision of what he wanted to create in terms of impact and empowered and trusted them. Our media team was inspired to go above and beyond.

When coworkers get to know each other, build strong relationships and evolve from teammates to friends, the irony is that they're not going the extra mile for the employer. They're doing it for their friends, people they care about, people they could never let down.

The more time I spent with the team, the more I realized how reliable everyone was. Remember Project Aristotle, which I discussed in chapter 5? It's the study that shed light on what makes teams successful at Google. While psychological safety comes first, a second element that is almost as important is the reliability of team members.[*]

---

[*] DUHIGG, Charles. What Google Learned from Its Quest to Build the Perfect Team. *New York Times Magazine*, 25 February 2016.

Being reliable includes being accountable for your work. It means getting the job done on time, every time, with the highest quality of work. In our team, it meant that the meals were ready, the coolers were full, the vehicles were filled.

Being reliable is contagious because no one wants to look bad. Doing your job well can have a significant impact in raising the standard of performance of the entire team, without having to say a word. Our actions and behaviors always speak for themselves.

Without undue pressure, we all wanted to go above and beyond for the mission. It was beautiful to see!

BRINGING THE TEAM TOGETHER

Each day Philippe and I took a few minutes to review the last 24 hours. The observation on day 2 was that energy was at its lowest since our arrival in Oceanside three days before departure. We were feeling the sleep deprivation of the bees, and the harsh reality of RAAM was starting to set in. The team needed a rallying cry now more than ever.

Philippe and I decided to gather the group for a huddle. The purpose of a huddle is to raise the energy level of the team and to explore ways to improve the situation for the coming days. It's no accident that the best Navy Seal units conduct a huddle after every combat operation. The exercise allows them to draw conclusions and adapt their methods for future missions.[*]

Philippe was my co-leader for the huddle. Philippe has a special ability to bring people together and everyone on the team loved him. He is an excellent communicator with a dynamic leadership style that complements my calm leadership. I knew I could count on him when I needed a rallying cry or to lighten the mood.

Philippe started the huddle with good news: "Everything is under control. We need to relax! We jumped 10 positions in the standings and

---

[*] WILLINK, Jocko, and BABIN, Leif. *Extreme Ownership: How US Navy SEALs Lead and Win*. St. Martin's Press, 2017.

went from 24th place to 14th today. The desert is starting to take its toll and there are already several dropouts from other teams."

A natural convener uses communication signals that inspire trust and reassure the team. Philippe can calm a team through his posture, gestures, and the tone, rhythm and intonation he uses when he speaks (para-verbal cues).[*]

I followed up his mini pep talk with a question for each person to answer: "What is your energy level from 1 to 10?" My intention was to take the overall pulse of the team. Some individuals mentioned sixes and sevens, which made me realize that I needed to do a better job of preserving the team's energy. The sleep strategy for the support team needed review. Currently, crew and vehicles were on the move too often; this didn't allow enough down time to rest. These reflections would help us develop a new sleep strategy for the team from day 4.

I followed up with two more questions: "What is going well so far, and what needs to change?" These questions are simple to answer and quickly identify areas to celebrate and areas for improvement. After only a few minutes, the huddle was over, and we had valuable information to make adjustments to improve our performance.

Philippe and I had neither planned nor discussed these huddles prior to departure. It was more of an ad hoc need that we identified from day 2. Throughout the race, we took other moments to bring the team together in the same way. Sometimes the huddles were in sub-teams in V1 or V2. In retrospect, it would have been easy to get distracted by our tasks and decide to skip these short debrief sessions. After all, we were all very busy and tired at the time of these meetings. However, this quick feedback exercise quickly became a team habit that strengthened our performance.

High-performing teams make space for strategic planning, regardless of how busy they are, because they understand that the success of the mission depends on being focused on the right tasks. In other words, high-performing teams understand the difference between urgent and

---

[*] DARIOLY, Annick, and SCHIMD MAST, Marianne. The Role of Nonverbal Behavior in Leadership: An Integrative Review. *Leader Interpersonal and Influence Skills*, Routledge/Taylor and Francis Group, 2013, pp. 73-100.

important and make room for both. They constantly analyze their results and measure their effectiveness to adapt their methods. This continuous feedback is a learning opportunity that allows for growth, quick adjustment in real time, and focus on the right actions.

BEING UBUNTU

When Sébastien woke up a few hours later, the school officials came to meet us. Before we arrived, they had prepared bags of ice, electrolyte drinks, snacks and a first aid kit for Sébastien. We were all very moved by their generosity. We were touched that a such an underprivileged school would give us so much.

This generosity made me think of the Ubuntu philosophy of South Africa. The Zulu term *Ubuntu* means to have humanity towards others. Nelson Mandela describes Ubuntu this way: "In the old days, when we were young, a traveler passing through a country would stop at a village and he did not have to ask for food or water. As soon as he stopped, people would give him what he needed."*

Leaving the village of Second Mesa, we passed through some very disadvantaged areas. Of all the RAAM, it was in these villages that we received the most encouragement from passersby and residents. People were waving, honking and really getting behind us. Later, when Sébastien recalled the story of the school, he reminded me of how much these people who had very little had touched him with their humanity.

I felt the spirit of Ubuntu in all these people. These moments remind me of the humanity that connects us all regardless of race, identity, religion or sexual orientation. Ubuntu invites us to focus on our commonalities rather than our differences.

By putting our energies into what brings us together, we open our horizons and create a better world. When we do so with our teammates, whom sometimes we do not choose, we create stronger and more resilient teams.

---

* BARTOLO, Samuel. The Concept of "Ubuntu" — Nelson Mandela. YouTube [online]. 5 December 2013. Available from: https://www.youtube.com/watch?v=D2lWQ6XvVgY

Souvenir photo with the Second Mesa Day School team. This moment will remain engraved in the memory of our team members as one of the most beautiful moments of the RAAM.

CHAPTER 10

BREAKING IN THE BEES

Sébastien Sasseville

Welcome to the bike's cockpit. You will now experience the first few days of the race from the cyclist's point of view. I'd say that days 1 through 3 were very challenging for the team. Until we found a routine that worked best and mastered our key performance moments, we were always on high alert. We were reacting and adapting; each new situation required us to think, analyze and act quickly to adjust and remain in the game.

I didn't see everything that was going on, but I was fully aware that the team was working hard to keep everything running. You could see it in their eyes, in the intensity of the conversations, in their attitude. I didn't know everything — in fact, I didn't know much, but I could sense their energy.

It was a hectic beginning: I saw my teammates running between the support vehicles, forgetting basic things, feeling apologetic; they were being put to the test. But I didn't ask questions; I had full confidence. It was obvious that everyone was giving their best effort, and that was all I asked. An imperfection should always be forgiven when one is doing their very best. Besides, they didn't need me to know when a mistake was made; they knew. And if they hadn't known, the joke would have been on me for failing to have prepared them adequately.

Anyway, I too was busy breaking into the process. I had promised myself to surrender to the team and obey orders. Inevitably, there were several times during the first few days when I interfered and tried to make some decisions about things that were not my business. One thing's for sure, once the real fatigue set in, I became much more docile!

THE SLEEP FACTOR

It may seem hard to believe, but upon arriving in Salome after 550 kilometers of cycling in 22 hours, I had a lot of trouble sleeping. We tried to work out what had happened, but in the end a combination of factors probably contributed to the very poor sleep. My body temperature was high and so was my heart rate. I could feel my heartbeat in my chest and in my head to the point that it kept me awake.

Beyond that, I am an extremely light sleeper. The slightest noise keeps me awake on a good day. My relationship with sleep was a big weakness during this first RAAM. It will definitely be one of the points to improve on for next time.

There was something very ironic about the first Seb to Bed. For the team, it was the big day, an opportunity to finally execute on this key moment for real. The team had prepared and rehearsed everything time and time again. All the equipment was meticulously organized, and every station I had to pass through was ready.

When I arrived, I felt like I was part of a military exercise. Not a second was wasted. There were never less than two of my team members helping me undress or eat, and their instructions were loud and clear. I could sense the team was filled with nervous energy. Once all the steps of one station were completed, I was hastily pulled to the next.

On paper, this was our best Seb to Bed of the entire race, executed to perfection in record time. The only problem was when I got to bed, my eyes were wide open! I had just been through a whirlwind that had completely woken me up and put me on high alert.

On the road, the refueling stations were always energizing. Interacting with my teammates helped me to get out of the solitude of the bike.

Philippe had the team well in hand. The refueling, whether done on the move from V1 or during a stop, was always perfect. All I had to do was stop and I was besieged by a group of bees who would refuel me in a few seconds, literally and figuratively.

As I left Salome, I shared with the team how the first Seb to Bed had felt and how it wired me. It felt funny, but it was important to communicate. This wasn't exactly easy to share, as the team had done everything perfectly. We agreed that the first Seb to Bed was effective, but the process could be a little mellower going forward. I didn't need any extra adrenaline before going to sleep.

When I left, I knew I was tackling another 500 kilometers without really having slept and recovered. I remember saying to Philippe, "It's going to take a magic trick to get through the day, but I know I'll be fine." Day 2 was starting, and I was already in a tight spot. I was confident that I had the resources to go the distance, but it was going to be imperative to get a good two hours of sleep the next day.

Gabriel has already given you a good recounting of our second stop at the Second Mesa Day School. He had the humility and the leadership to trust the team to find a solution to a problem when he was outside his zone of genius. The team was resourceful in finding me a place to sleep, and when I walked into the Second Mesa Day School gym, as eloquently recounted by Gabriel in the previous chapter, everything was perfect. My bed was set up in the corner, Manon was ready to take care of my insulin pump, Marie-Michèle was waiting for me with her therapy table, and my rest clothes were in the bathroom. But when I arrived and saw a two-inch-thick mattress in the corner of a gym, the voice in my head immediately said, "There's no way I'm going to be able to sleep here."

Maintenance personnel passed through the gym a few times. Philippe lay a few feet away from me, breathing noisily. My heart rate was still elevated. Despite a thousand kilometers in two days, and 60 minutes of sleep at the previous stop, I didn't sleep a wink at the school.

To this day, I am almost embarrassed. How could I be surrounded by so much kindness and not be able to fall asleep? Why did my body refuse to sleep? When I got up, I was miserable. I left the school around 6 p.m. It was still very hot, and for the third time we had the goal of covering

450 to 500 kilometers. This time I told Philippe: "I don't know how I'm going to make it, but I will . . ."

HOUSTON, WE HAVE A PROBLEM

Another major challenge was emerging before us. RAAM has three time cut-offs within the overall distance. If you don't reach these checkpoints in time, you are eliminated immediately and your race is over.

The first checkpoint was in Durango, Colorado. We had to be there before 9 p.m. local time on June 17, 81 hours and 1,500 kilometers after the start of the race. I never anticipated that the first cut-off would be an issue. After all, I was in great shape. I could hold my own among the best athletes in the world, and we were certainly hoping to finish in the top 10 of the race.

The five-hour break in Salome and my lack of sleep created a whole new reality. There was now a real possibility of not making it on time. Day 3 was extremely difficult. I was way more fatigued than I should have been at this point in the race. I arrived in Cortez mid-afternoon with 75 kilometers separating us from Durango. Plenty of time remained, but I had been riding for 21 hours and it was time to stop for sleep. One thing was extremely clear to everyone: our race depended on my next sleep break.

In the discussions we had after our return home from RAAM, everyone was unanimous. One of the moments I seemed the lowest was at the end of day 3. My eyes were completely blank. I was completely absent. We all expected this, but certainly not on day 3.

This Seb to Bed routine was still very effective but much more peaceful and less military than before. I remember that Gabriel was the last to leave the room. He wished me goodnight, but we both knew what that meant: "Sleep or it's over."

Thank God, I slept like a baby. After 1,500 kilometers in three days, and with only 60 minutes of cumulative sleep, my body finally agreed to rest. I fell into a deep sleep the second I put my head on the pillow. The team found me in the same position they had left me. I slept for two and a half hours.

Sleep had gone well, but nothing was won yet. That's what RAAM is all about. It's 10, 11 or 12 days in a row on your bike, 20 to 22 hours a day, and nothing else. Not a single break, not a day of rest. Before the finish line, the wins are small and always followed by dozens of hours of suffering on the bike. If you stop for more than two or three hours a day, you won't make it across the continent on time. You'll come home with a DNF (did not finish), and everything you've done will have been for nothing.

As usual, as soon as I opened my eyes, it was all hands on deck. I didn't have an alarm to wake me up — a teammate always came in and got me underway. I did not have a cellphone, neither did I have a room key. The team decided how long I would sleep. I was completely in their hands.

Manon would arrive with breakfast and set up my insulin pump for the day. Clean bike clothes had been left in the room a few hours earlier, when the Seb to Bed was prepared. Martin was waiting outside the motel door, holding the bike. Philippe, the driver and the navigator were already in V1, behind the bike, ready to go on my first pedal stroke.

Even if this kind of endurance event is punctuated by many discomforts (to put it mildly), waking up and getting going was by far the most difficult moment. Fatigue accumulates day after day. Sometimes you have to fight to stay awake on the bike, so when you wake up in a warm bed, far from recovered, still trashed and overly sleep-deprived, it's incredibly difficult to get moving. Not only do you have to get out of bed, but you have to be in performance mode immediately. Fifteen minutes later, you're on the bike. It can be hot or cold, sunny or rainy. Sore muscles need to warm up slowly. You have to deal with traffic and take orders from the navigator. And that "morning"— in fact, it was 5 p.m. — a strong performance was imperative. The infamous cut-off was 75 kilometers ahead. I had to get on the bike and get to work. I had four hours.

Normally, this wouldn't have been a concern, as any average cyclist can cover 75 kilometers in two to three hours. But in the context of RAAM, average speeds are much slower and anything can happen. The course also had some pretty significant climbs. Given my state of fatigue, the challenge was considerable.

The first pedal strokes of the day are always very telling. It is at this moment that we can see if the "night" was restorative, what the general state of the cyclist is and what kind of performance we can expect in the next 24 hours.

After a few kilometers on the bike on the way to Durango, I felt well. My first "real night" had really helped. The course started with a few climbs, which I got through very quickly. Everything indicated that we would be in Durango on time. Morale was also very good, and I remember having some great conversations with the team.

I had certainly had my doubts earlier in the day, but I didn't express them, as I didn't want to worry the team. I had simply promised that we would get there. On paper, we had the time, and, despite the tight deadline, I felt I had the energy. But still, given the sleep issues of the first few days and the fact that I never thought I would be in a precarious position so early in the race, I had my doubts.

Doubts are healthy and normal. In fact, the size of your doubts is proportional to the size of your ambitions. When the bar is set very high, you can expect the road to be filled with a lot of questioning.

It's almost as if the universe wants to make sure you are convinced that you've chosen the right path. A leader has the right to doubt. That said, I didn't doubt the mission and its importance. I just had a momentary doubt about my ability to complete it. It was because of that doubt that I redoubled my efforts, focused on doing all the right things and didn't go on autopilot.

JUST BECAUSE IT'S BAD DOESN'T MEAN IT'S NOT GOOD

Moving towards Durango, even though I was going at a good pace, the ride still felt very difficult. It was hard, but it was going well. Just because things are hard doesn't mean it's not going well.

I have certainly repeated this phrase many times in my journey. I first came up with it many years ago while going through some difficulties. I was again facing challenges, but all in all, I was headed in the right direction. The bigger the goal, the more challenges there will be — that's the nature of these projects. Earlier that day, Philippe had come up to me to see how I was doing. With a huge smile I said, "It's really hard! I've never suffered so much!" and we both had a big laugh.

This moment is engraved in our memory — it's a highlight of the trip. It was full of humor, self-deprecation and an admission that you must be a little deranged to do this race. But I had chosen to be there *precisely* because it was one of the hardest races in the world, so I might as well find a way to enjoy it.

How do we learn to make sense of things? How do we become able to objectively identify what's going well and what needs to be improved? How do we keep moving forward while remaining positive? How do we deal with difficult moments within our teams? Like everything else, it's by practicing. It's a matter of asking ourselves simple questions, such as what's going well, what do I have control of, what's going wrong, am I going in the right direction? And then, very simply again, we can take action to correct what's going wrong, or at least improve things bit by bit. Typically, things are better than we think, and in the end, we have to remember that nothing is perfect.

It's important to learn to focus on the positive and to accept a certain degree of imperfection. That's an important quality for an endurance athlete, because when you've been riding or running for 12 hours, your brain is good at finding a perfectly valid reason to stop. That's protection mechanism. Good endurance athletes can continue moving forward despite some imperfection and discomfort.

Optimism is also an important quality for an endurance athlete. Optimism isn't an attribute, it's a habit.

Like any habit, it can be improved. Here's a three-step process to help you be more optimistic:

Stop.

Scan.

Adjust.

Stop and take a pause to think more clearly, scan and inspect your current posture and attitude and then adjust your posture. When you choose the posture, be selfish. Choose a posture that is going to serve you in achieving your goal.

Sometimes I hear people say "I'm having a bad day," and it is 10 a.m.! There seems to be room for things to turn around and get better. Stop, scan, adjust.

I am often asked if I like to suffer. The answer is not at all! When I am asked this question, I feel like we are looking at the same mountain but from completely different vantage points. Obviously, we are not seeing the same thing. I don't see the discomforts. Rather, I see what I'm learning; I see the skills and resilience I'm gaining, the life-changing experiences I am accumulating, the impact of my actions on others. This is how pain is transformed into happiness.

I have been in situations that forced me to think this way as a matter of survival. I always try to apply the behaviors I learned during these sporting events to everyday situations. During a race, I put my emotions aside. I try to detach myself from the situation and observe what is happening to find solutions. I have a very pragmatic, logical and emotion-free approach to problem solving. It is about being able to put what's going well and what's not going so well in two separate boxes, instead of only feeling one emotion, which is often negative when things aren't going our way.

LITTLE THINGS THAT CHANGE EVERYTHING

When you go from theory to reality, you realize that there are many small things that make a big difference — things that can only be experienced in real life.

Around Durango, after a few climbs, a new energy seized me. Physically and psychologically, I was refreshed. With the climbs behind us, I had great hope that I could reach the checkpoint in time.

What happened on the road to Durango? Little things. Vi came to my side, and Philippe told me he had some good news. More racers had dropped out, consequently moving me up in the rankings. Everyone was smiling and motivated. They joked with me and kept me entertained. They gave me a brownie, one of my favorite snacks. The view was beautiful.

My mental and physical posture was completely transformed. Motivation came back, and my legs were reborn. I was smiling and making jokes, and my pace increased.

This happened several times during the race — a small thing that has a big impact. A tipping point that changes everything. Sometimes it was a word, a joke or a funny event, or even a stressful one that put everyone back on alert. Overtaking another racer with confidence. Those little things that change everything are real gifts. We never know when they're going to happen, and they happen only on one condition: you must be there. You must take a first step, commit, be in the moment, move forward and relentlessly pursue your goal.

Being in the right place at the right time — it happens much more often when we take action.

You certainly have to be sensitive to the little things, and that, too, is an art. You have to keep your antennas up, because with our fast-paced lives, it's easy to pass them by. When we are in a state of extreme exhaustion, it's amazing how simple things make us happy. A doughnut, dry clothes, a cold-water bottle — they warm the heart! In this state of extreme fragility, we return to the essentials, and happiness comes easy. We notice the caring gestures of others. My extreme state of fatigue created a vulnerability that heightened my sense of gratitude. This complete dependence on others turned out to be a beautiful experience, one that I wish for each and every one of you.

THE PRACTICE OF RESILIENCE

Through other challenges completed prior to RAAM, I had learned one particularly important thing: resilience is not a personality trait; it is a practice.

Resilience is something you train, like a muscle. It's built during all the small acts of daily life. Going for a run even if it's raining. Getting up 30 minutes early for work. Adapting to the unexpected with a smile. It's the small, voluntary, daily acts of resilience that serve to build resilience strong enough to handle the hardships we don't choose.

The push to Durango went wonderfully, and we finally reached the checkpoint at 8:30 p.m., a full 30 minutes before the cut-off. It was night, so V1 was following me, and we talked via radio. I admitted to the team that in the afternoon, I had had doubts. For me, promising the team that we would make it was my way to try to motivate everyone. Everyone in V1 had a good laugh, saying, "Don't worry, we had doubts too!" Clearly, they didn't need me to motivate themselves.

Fatigue was getting the better of me, and my cognitive abilities were diminishing further by the hour. I really wished I could be there for all of them, but very soon I was going to be a zombie that they would have to manage.

AN EARLY SENSE OF URGENCY

In hindsight, and now that I understand my sleep and its limitations better, the ideal strategy for me would have been to ride 30, 35 or 40 consecutive hours after the start. However, this approach requires an impeccable cooling strategy in the desert. It must be said that historically, this is the approach of most participants who aspire to a podium.

RAAM is a process of exhaustion of resources and participants. Whoever dreams of finishing this race must understand that consistency is king. But "consistent" does not mean "no fatigue." Like it or not, even the most consistent athlete will show a gradual decrease in average speed. In the final days, there is no more attack or acceleration possible. There's nothing left in the legs, and every cyclist just grinds it out.

This highlights an important lesson. One hundred kilometers on day 2 is not the same as 100 kilometers on day 9. There is a world of difference between the two. On day 2, you can still accelerate, attack and catch up. On day 9, 100 kilometers behind is impossible to make up.

An early sense of urgency is a great predicator of performance. Go out strong, build a gap and win the race.

A sense of urgency is good, but having it early in the race is what separates you from the pack. In business or in a race, everyone feels a sense of urgency towards the deadline — that's easy. It can be the end of a race, or a few days before a project delivery date, or a sales quota towards the end of a fiscal year. If we wait until the last few moments to go full throttle, it is often too late.

To win and rise above the fray, you need a sense of urgency early in the race. This means making gains as early as possible, not waiting to jump in, not procrastinating, not relying on future performance. The earlier the sense of urgency, the better the performance.

I find that the best way to create a sense of urgency early in a process is to break the whole task down into smaller chunks and give them a timeframe for completion. By doing this, you quickly realize that there is often less time than you think, and that you need to get started immediately.

In this way, the interdependence of each work block is quickly brought to light. If another business unit has to take over or needs a deliverable to do its part, we have to deliver ours on time. If not, the whole chain automatically falls behind.

This exercise also reveals once more the importance of consistency. It's the early efforts that allow you to move forward at a steady and balanced pace and potentially avoid doing everything at the last minute.

CHAPTER 11

PUSHING THROUGH ADVERSITY

Sébastien Sasseville

Celebrations at the Durango checkpoint were very brief — nearly non-existent. At all time stations, each team is required to register online on the RAAM electronic platform. This was done en route by the V1 navigator. I was notified that I had passed the checkpoint via radio and continued on my way without stopping. When you tackle RAAM, the celebrations are for the end. If you finish.

With the checkpoint behind us, the task ahead was still monumental. After all, I was just entering the fourth night and the finish line was still more than 3,000 kilometers away. This night would be quite punishing.

Shortly after the checkpoint, I was attacking the mountains of Colorado in darkness and rain. Twenty-four hours earlier, I was suffocating in the Arizona desert. Now I was on another planet. Vegetation was abundant, the trees were gigantic, and I felt the cold for the first time. In fact, I had to make several stops to put on warmer clothes. Guided by the lights of V1, I made my way in the pouring rain, all night, mostly uphill.

In our post-RAAM discussions, Philippe and Gabriel admitted to me that they would've had to be paid a lot of money to switch roles with me that night. Looking back, that night was horrible. The conditions were awful, my discomfort level high. From the outside, it was terrible. However, I have good memories of it. I did what I had to do without questioning it; I wanted to be there, I had chosen to be there. I knew there would be rainy nights and I was where I wanted to be. To tell you the truth, I didn't think too much about it in the moment. I had to ride, so I rode. It was the only way to get to the finish line.

With 1,500 kilometers in my legs, a cumulative sleep of just three and a half hours and with another 450-kilometer chunk before the next two-hour sleep, I pedaled. I was in the experience; what I was doing did not seem abnormal at the time. Today, looking back, I can see that there was nothing normal about the situation. But what I retained from this experience is that when you launch into something, the fear of uncertainty goes away, and you instinctively do what you need to do.

Once in the action, after the first steps, what had been a scary future reality quickly becomes the new normal. This new reality is no longer frightening, it's no longer strange or terrible. One should never look at a future reality through the lenses of the present, because the challenges of that future will appear insurmountable.

SURREAL MOMENTS

Our RAAM experience had no shortage of surreal moments. One of them was particularly memorable. It was when I was doing my business in a bucket . . . while receiving a shoulder massage from my brother-in-law, Martin . . . while on the edge of the highway.

And it seemed normal to us.

Obviously, this isn't normal! But this was our reality, a new reality that no longer frightened us, or at least a new reality that we didn't question. We were in the moment, every minute counted, and we executed without questioning. Of course, while this scene was unfolding, there was a moment when we all paused. Someone jokingly said, "Wow, when you think about it, this is a little weird!" We laughed, but it didn't change what we had to do.

We always added a few tablespoons of coconut oil to my water bottles to increase my calorie intake. Again, a not-so-normal action that became normal during RAAM. I wouldn't do that now, but then it was our reality.

When we face a new challenge and hesitate to dive in, we focus on the potential obstacles, the pain, the possibility of failure, the scenarios where we don't have the required expertise. We imagine the moments when we will "shit the bed," or in the bucket — and that can be scary. Too often, these concerns become excuses for not getting started. But the truth is, it's our survival instinct at work. These doubts are a protective mechanism, and sometimes you have to learn to work around it.

If you have ever run a marathon, you know that once the marathon starts, especially if it's your first, your stress immediately dissipates. When we embrace the moment, when we accept starting without having all the answers, we create a space for our resilience to emerge. When we take the plunge — those first courageous steps — the new reality quickly becomes the new normal. Our worries dissolve, and we find solutions to the problems that arise. The body and mind acclimatize to the new environment, and we develop new habits and expertise. All this, provided we take a first step.

How do we build resilience? Wrong question. Everyone has resilience, but we don't always know how to tap into it.

My journey has taught me one thing. When we have no choice, we are always resilient. Talk to people diagnosed with a serious illness, or refugees who choose to walk thousands of miles to find a better life. To be human is to be resilient. Each of us is resilient, but we don't always express this resilience.

The problem is that our modern societies offer an abundance of escape routes in all areas of our lives. These alternatives offer us another option to making an effort and demonstrating resilience. Humans, naturally programmed to avoid discomfort, very often choose the easy option.

But in reality, no one lacks resilience — resilience is our survival instinct. To exercise it, we simply have to choose to do difficult things. To express our resilience, and leverage it to grow, learn and improve, we must willingly put ourselves in tough situations.

CREATING AN IRREVERSIBLE COMMITMENT

To exercise resilience, we must commit to a situation in an irreversible way. Create a situation where we have no choice but to succeed.

An often overlooked aspect of these large projects is the planning and preparation phase. Take the story we're telling here. We've recounted much of the action to prepare for and to get through RAAM, but there is still a large part that is behind the scenes. For example, its financing.

The total cost of our RAAM was $100,000. Of course, it is possible to do RAAM on a smaller budget. You don't necessarily need a trailer, a photographer, a videographer and a social media professional. A team of six to eight people is enough. However, a minimum budget of $50,000 is a necessity. A notice to interested parties!

I registered for RAAM in July 2021. The registration fee was US$3,750. This was my irreversible commitment. I had committed to myself that I would do whatever it took to find the funding. Twelve months in advance, before I had even recruited the team, I spent several weeks preparing offers to potential sponsors. As usual, the hunt for sponsors was arduous. You have to personalize each offer, work to get many meetings to sell the project, negotiate, build customized campaigns — and be prepared to receive 10 noes for every yes.

In my mind, I never considered the possibility that I wouldn't get the funding. In fact, I didn't leave myself any choice. I was signed up and committed. I was telling everyone around me that in 2022, I would be racing RAAM. That's where resilience comes from. Not having a choice.

Creating an irreversible commitment can be as simple as signing up for a 10-kilometer race when you don't yet have the fitness to do it. Signing up for an online course. Opening a bank account for your new business. The first step can be extremely small, and it should be within reach. At this stage, you don't have to get everything perfect, you just need to initiate movement.

In the end, what's essential to remember is that the first step is the hardest but the most powerful. The trick to getting started is to get started.

DARKNESSES ALWAYS PASSES

After I reached the checkpoint in Colorado, the hours passed one after another until the sun returned with the morning. My journey has taught me one more thing: darkness always passes.

I am often asked how to overcome obstacles, how to bounce back and self-motivate during difficult times. Sometimes it's not about overcoming obstacles, it's about welcoming them. After all, why would I want to leave when the professor arrives? Meeting obstacles is the only thing that is guaranteed when you set ambitious goals. In fact, setting the bar high is saying, "I choose the obstacles." So why are we so eager to get past them when they arise?

During RAAM, energy is cyclical. The same goes for motivation and fatigue. On the bike, from start to finish, I experienced, or endured, these cycles. For three or four hours, no matter what time of the day or night, I could go through a cycle where both energy and motivation were high. That was always followed with its opposite — a cycle with no energy and lower motivation. Each cycle had its own duration, and each day's pattern was different.

Moments of strength and positive energy can be taken over at any time by challenging periods filled with difficulty, and vice versa.

As endurance athletes, our ability to get through a cycle where morale is lower and the body is weaker is directly related to our performance and ability to finish the race. The best endurance athletes are the ones who get good at getting through dark times.

During a difficult cycle, it's important to get back to basics. In my case, it was about staying well hydrated and fueling adequately. You also must accept that you have to slow down. The body is sending you a message that it needs to repair itself, so if we try to push it faster, we will only break it further. When hitting a rough patch, we must go into a place of love and self-care, rather than frustration and self-flagellation. Here I see an interesting parallel between sports and our professional lives.

Those who have trained for a half or full marathon are aware of the concept of periodizing one's training. In fact, whether you are a cyclist, triathlete or athlete in general, you'll find the same principle in most training programs.

Periodization is the creation of cycles where the volume and intensity of training increases from week to week, followed by a week of rest. This week has a significant decrease in the volume and intensity of exercise. Athletes always welcome the rest week. It's not perceived as an obstacle to performance; on the contrary, all athletes know that recovery is essential to improving performance.

However, too often in our professional lives, we try to be at 100 percent (and sometimes even at 120 percent) of our capacities 100 percent of the time. This pace isn't sustainable, and it's certainly not conducive to good performance. (In the next chapter, Gabriel will tell a wonderful story that illustrates the importance of periodically disconnecting to create better performance.)

During RAAM, I experienced many dark times. I've certainly had them before in my other sporting experiences; but there are dark moments, and then there is RAAM darkness. In fact, these were some of the most difficult moments I have experienced in my life.

During each difficult cycle, I tried to take an observer's perspective. This allowed me to focus on solutions. I didn't want a difficult period to negatively impact my confidence level or general mental outlook. I said it earlier — we can stay highly motivated, even when things are going very badly. We can be convinced that we'll succeed even during the darkest times.

This ability to navigate through tough times is important in our organizations. On a bike or in business attire, this means forgetting about the finish line and focusing on the right actions, habits and behaviors. Continuous learning, rigorous client follow-up, adequate preparation before a meeting, doing what we said we would do — whatever this means in your professional life. Doing the basics right isn't sexy, but it works. We often become obsessed with our objectives and goals. Ironically, and especially when we encounter adversity, we need to forget about the endgame and focus on what's needed in the moment to eventually get us there.

Patience and humility are important values to cultivate to get through dark times. Forgetting the finish line and focusing on the right actions isn't always glamorous and it demands that we roll up our sleeves. We need patience because the results we seek often take time. The good news is that the right actions and habits bring lasting results and ensure long-term success.

CHAPTER 12

REST IN MOTION

Gabriel Renaud

RAAM, for Sébastien as well as for the entire team, was a 12-day nonstop effort. Until day 4, there was little to no break time for the team. We were on the road every day doing what we do best, being bees. There was no time for periodization. No time for a rest day.

Bees are great people to have on a team. They are reliable, responsible, adaptable and able to respond to new demands quickly. They are not difficult to lead and are always ready for a new challenge. They are loyal to the mission and to their teammates.

However, bees have a potentially serious flaw: they can sometimes forget themselves and get burned out.

I had been warned of the difficulty of the role I was taking on. A few days before the start, I went to register the team. I had the chance to talk to one of the race organizers, who had also been a crew chief in a previous year. He was a bee and gave too much of himself in that role. With the best intentions of going the extra mile to support his rider and team, he neglected his sleep and broke down in the final days. His team had to take over most of his responsibilities. This testimony really stuck with me and was a great reminder to respect my limits.

PUT YOUR OXYGEN MASK ON FIRST

This discussion with the race organizer reminded me of a well-known concept highlighted by the author Kevin N. Lawrence: "Put your oxygen mask on first." In other words, you can't help others if you don't take care of yourself first.*

In our context, this meant "The better I am, the better we are." From the moment we arrived in Oceanside, everyone was responsible for their individual well-being while considering the collective good. Before departure, because there were so many tasks to complete, the bees got up at 6 a.m. The first thing we would do was go for a jog or an outdoor workout.

During RAAM, I encouraged each person to take a moment to exercise during the day to raise their energy level. Over and over during RAAM, I saw team members going for a run, doing roadside exercises, and, when we had the luxury of a hotel, going to the gym or pool. Martin was always the first to jump into the pool, and he usually dragged the rest of the team with him.

Putting on our oxygen mask first was also about eating well to maintain good energy levels. Some of the team members had supported Sébastien during his bike ride across Canada the previous year. Due to a lack of resources and planning, the team was forced to eat junk food and to do their grocery shopping at gas stations. They said they gained 10 pounds in 10 days! I didn't want us to make the same mistake. Eat junk food for 12 days and you'll see your body fall apart.

Finally, putting your oxygen mask on first includes the ability to ask for help with humility. For example, one team member told me that he didn't want to do night shifts. He had a bad back that wouldn't allow him to sit in the van without moving for that long. In addition, he admitted that he was a light sleeper who could easily fall prey to sleep deprivation. It was a great demonstration of humility, self-awareness and even courage, considering we had a team of young Vikings who were not afraid of 20-hour days.

---

* LAWRENCE, Kevin N. *Your Oxygen Mask First: 17 Habits to Help High Achievers Survive & Thrive in Leadership & Life*. Lioncrest, 2017.

If this individual had not spoken up for fear of the judgment of others, the whole team would have suffered. In the end, this individual shone during the day in the role he was assigned.

This is something I took pride in as a leader: the reconciliation of performance with team well-being. Yes, we had a culture where performance was important, but well-being always took precedence. In fact, well-being and performance are interrelated. It's not individualistic to put your oxygen mask on first; it's a gesture that allows us to better rise together.

By this point in the race, I had worked four consecutive night shifts. As team leader, I was constantly in demand day and night, so I slept very little during those first four days. Since our arrival in Oceanside, my partner, Valérie, and I had not had any time together. In short, my head and my body needed a moment of disconnection and rejuvenation, and my spirit needed to escape as well. I needed to get out of this performance routine for a short while. That's when we arrived in the small village of La Veta.

MAKE ROOM FOR SPONTANEITY

La Veta is a small town of 1,900 people located in the mountains of Colorado, and Sébastien was going to stop there for a sleep break. After

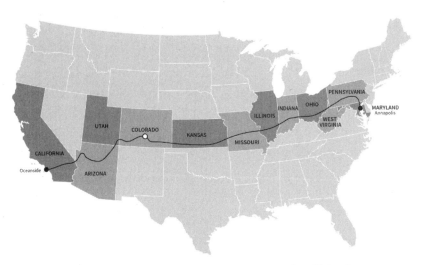

Location of the village of La Veta, nestled in the mountains of Colorado.

a fourth Seb to Bed, we were a well-oiled machine; our fluidity and ability to execute was impressive. Knowing that most of the next day's tasks were already completed, and with the agreement of the team, I asked Valérie to come spend some time with me in La Veta.

The village is beautiful and ended up being a great place to have a short getaway to escape the intensity of the race. The whole team was aware that we were experiencing RAAM as a couple and that it was a special experience for us. The team had given us 90 minutes, not one more!

I suggested to Valérie that we go to a café on the main street. As we entered a little bar with an art boutique, a man noticed that we were wearing identical sweaters. Approaching us enthusiastically, he said, "I feel like there's a story behind these shirts!" We replied that we were participating in a bike race across the United States and briefly explained what it was all about. We felt like we were talking to the owner of the place. However, we soon discovered that he and his wife were customers.

This man, Daniel, invited us to sit at the bar to continue the conversation with him and his wife. After about 30 minutes of conversation, Valérie shared that we were taking a moment away from the team to come and recharge as a couple. She explained how intense RAAM is and how important this little recovery break was.

Daniel replied: "Have you ever had the serenade sung?" I turned to Valérie: "Do you know what a serenade is?" She answered: "Yes, it's a song!"

Daniel then led us into an adjacent room, behind the café. We discovered a stage with about 50 chairs arranged theater-style. There were some instruments on the stage, including a grand piano. Daniel invited us to take a seat in the front row.

Here we were, Valérie and I, enjoying a private concert in a small theater in a bucolic village. After a few notes, it was clear that Daniel was a professional. He began singing, and he crafted a song about the history of the village of La Veta.

He sang about the river, the mountains and the village café. As the song progressed, he made us part of the story. He sang about two lovers coming to the café, who were accompanying a cyclist doing something impossible. I don't remember the exact words, but I do remember a phrase that stuck with me: "Tell your cyclist that I say hello and that the mountains of La Veta will carry him to the finish line."

Daniel continued to play for about 10 minutes. His eyes were piercing; it was clear that he was very sensitive and had great emotional intelligence. Valérie took my hand and cried tears of joy; it was so beautiful! Daniel finished his song and looked us straight in the eyes.

We had just lived an incredibly unique and special moment. A simple impromptu outing that became an unforgettable memory. After a bit more conversation with Daniel, we thanked him from the bottom of our hearts. It was now time to go back.

Two hours after putting him to bed, it was time to wake Sébastien up. As I got him ready, I shared with him what we had experienced, especially the words "The mountains of La Veta will carry you to the finish line." Sébastien, under the effect of fatigue, burst into tears. Poor guy! He was starting to become quite fragile.

When we left the camp, Sébastien wasn't feeling too well. The day started with a long and difficult climb. I don't know how much magic the mountains of La Veta worked that day, but one pedal stroke at a time, for over an hour, much slower than his usual pace, he ascended in silence. Once at the top, Sébastien came back to life and had one of his best sequences on the bike.

ADAPTING THE SLEEP STRATEGY

At the risk of seeming repetitious, extreme sleep deprivation is, without a doubt, the biggest challenge of RAAM. Sure, my head was now rested, but my body was still tired.

Initially, the sleep strategy for the RV team was to stop at public places like malls and gas stations. After a few days, we realized that plan wouldn't work. With the equipment and luggage, we didn't have enough space or beds in the RV. The heat was also greatly reducing the quality of our sleep. As a result, we decided that everyone would sleep in the comfort of a hotel room. A tired crew put everyone's safety at risk, and that was unacceptable.

The first go-round of this new strategy was not perfect. By renting a hotel room at the same location as the Seb to Bed, where Seb slept late into the afternoon, the team that was off at night had to get up at 3 a.m. to drive 200 kilometers forward to meet Sébastien and the V1 crew for the 7 a.m. start of the day shift. These short nights were inefficient and not very restorative.

On day 4, starting from the village of La Veta, Dan had the idea to book a hotel room halfway ahead of Sébastien and his next stop.

Yes, Dan again, solving a problem with a simple but creative solution. The RV team was now sleeping at the Seb to Bed and traveling only once a day, about 450 kilometers. The RV team had more downtime, which made Manon's job in the kitchen easier. The V2 team, on the other hand, was now going to sleep halfway through the next day's journey, about 225 kilometers further on, so approximately at the same place as the morning team change. Since we were already at the meeting point in the morning, this allowed for longer nights and much better sleep.

This small strategy optimization had a big impact on the energy levels of the team. For me, La Veta was the first night since the start that I was not on board V1. That night, I slept a good six hours. The impact was immediate. The next day I was as fresh as a daisy. In the following days, I observed a more energized, relaxed and smiling team. In the end, being willing and able to try new strategies, and being highly adaptable and able to pivot quickly had a big impact on our performance. It is important that we don't fall in love with our strategy and that we are always able to question it.

STEPPING OUT OF THE GAME

In V1, we were always on high alert, like athletes on the field. Those first few days in the chase vehicle taught me that the brain never stops as long as it's in the game. In V1, we had to be prepared to react at any moment, quickly making decisions and executing. You can't rest in a high-stress environment like this one. This constant stimulation made me realize the importance of periodically getting out of the game. These moments allow us to psychologically detach ourselves from the work and contribute to our well-being; but, most importantly, they help us maintain a high level of performance when we get back to work.

Following a cyclist during the day, driving 20 to 25 km/h, is a feat in itself; imagine doing it at night. It seemed impossible for one driver to stay alert for all those hours, so we rotated between drivers, navigators and even the sports director. These shifts allowed us to take power snoozes of 30 to 45 minutes.

These naps were taken in the back of V1 in a small area set up for this purpose. Jokingly, this tiny corner adjacent to the back seat was dubbed the master bedroom. This five-star room allowed us to complete the night shift safely with the required vigilance.

Still, it took a few days to find the right recipe to create truly restorative breaks.

Initially, it was virtually impossible to take a nap without being woken up. The coolers and the rest of the food storage were only accessible from the back seat, right next to the mattress set up for our naps. Since Sébastien usually ate and drank every 20 to 30 minutes, we were in demand even during our rest breaks.

Interestingly, we were always awakened by an internal "alarm" triggered by certain words heard during sleep, even before the navigator or driver made any request. Our communication system allowed us to hear Sébastien through the car's speakers. As you can imagine, as soon as Sébastien made a request with words associated with our execution and performance, such as *soda, brownie, blood sugar* or *diabetes*, our subconscious would wake us up. Think back to a time when you woke up with a start. It's quite unpleasant! That's what we experienced every time one of those words was spoken.

And if Sébastien's request didn't wake us up, you can be sure that the driver and navigator would get you moving by your first name: "Gab, I need a bottle!"

We were always on our toes, always on the alert. After a few days, we started to know and anticipate Sébastien's needs. So, before the sports director went for a nap, he would provide some drinks and snacks for the driver and the navigator to have up front so that they would not disturb his precious sleep. Philippe became an expert at anticipating Sébastien's diabetes needs. With experience, he usually managed to stay two steps ahead, allowing us much more peaceful rests in the second half of the race.

All this helped me realize that there are times to be in the game, and moments when we should actively take a break. Our hyper-connected world creates an environment where constant productivity is valued, and moments of respite are rare. Even on our vacations, we are sometimes bombarded with communication of one sort or another. Hence the importance of intentionally and fully stepping out of the game, as I did at La Veta. Philippe chose not to do so, which probably amplified my realization.

Philippe, as the sports director, saw his role as mission critical and challenged himself to spend 100 percent of the race in V1, except for the few hours that Sébastien slept. Not surprisingly, at some point, his performance was affected. This was true for the whole team as days went by, but we were getting a few more hours of sleep than Philippe and had the luxury of spending long periods away from the intensity of V1.

Yes, Philippe has an out-of-this-world stamina, energy and drive. But at the end of the race, he confessed to me that this high-pressure environment was slowly burning him out. This admission highlighted the importance of voluntary disconnection for performance and our well-being.

Even with the greatest determination and resilience in the world, the brain needs time to recover. In fact, research indicates that mentally stepping away from work for a vacation, a weekend or just an evening is directly linked to well-being, greater life satisfaction and fewer burnouts.[*] But despite what the research says, the reality for many is that it's hard to exit the game. The hustle and bustle of everyday life sucks us in, and we sometimes forget ourselves amid all the tasks we must get done.

A few years ago, I discovered a powerful statistic about the probability of achieving a goal. I hope this statistic will be as useful to you as it was to me in taking a break from the game more often. Yes, taking time off is also something we need to treat as a goal, and a goal just as important as our performance.

In this study, researchers calculated the probability of achieving a goal according to the frame of mind one has towards it.[**]

---

[*] FRITZ, Charlotte, ELLIS, Allison M., DEMSKY, Caitlin A., *et al*. Embracing Work Breaks. *Organizational Dynamics*, 2013, vol. 42, no. 4, pp. 274-280.

[**] NEWLAND, Stephen. The Power of Accountability. AFCPE [online]. 27 November 2018. Available from: https://www.afcpe.org/news-and-publications/the-standard/2018-3/the-power-of-accountability/.

What is this probability of success?

- 10% if you hear an idea;
- 25% if you consciously decide to adopt it;
- 40% if you decide when to do it;
- 50% if you plan how to do it;
- 65% if you commit to another person;
- 95% if you have an accountability meeting with the person to whom you made the commitment.

To allow yourself more time to disconnect, good intentions are not always enough. We're all seeking balance, yet few of us can claim that we have achieved this goal. To successfully disconnect and recharge, you need to make it a clear and quantified goal, decide when to do it and plan how to do it. As the research cited above shows, the best way to do this is to make a pledge to another person. That is, whether it is with colleagues, friends or partners, you hold each other accountable to voluntarily step out of the game and disconnect, for greater performance.

PART III

ALWAYS MOVING

Life isn't about waiting for the storm to pass . . .
It's about learning to dance in the rain.

— VIVIEN GREENE, AUTHOR

CHAPTER 13

ADAPT OR DIE

Gabriel Renaud

Everything was going relatively well for team 661, and Sébastien was now in 12th place. At this point in the race, you might think that everything was under control. Except for a few unforeseen events, we were like a family of ducks placidly crossing a lake. However, underwater, we ducks were working hard. We were moving our legs relentlessly to keep up the pace and reach the destination on time.

The finish line was still a long way off. More than 3,000 kilometers to go, and at any time, everything could change in one way or another. So far, there had been a few bumps in the road, but nothing major that required a reworking of the plan.

Let's quickly go back a few days before continuing our journey. Recall our second stop at the Second Mesa Day School on the Hopi Reservation. When we left the school, we had a big day ahead of us, both in terms of distance and elevation gain. Sébastien had to reach the first cut-off in Durango on time. The challenge had energized us, and we were all completely dialed in. Still, we were unprepared for the hand life was about to deal us.

Soon after leaving the school, the V1 crew — Réjean, Philippe, and I — received a serious message from Sébastien regarding a situation with his diabetes. A night from hell was about to begin. Something we had never planned for during our simulations would require us to adapt every minute.

SLOW DOWN TO GO FASTER

I left an audio message in the team's group chat: "Hi everyone, I have news from Sébastien. His morale is good. However, his blood sugar is at 18. We've been trying to get it down for about two hours, but it's not working. We injected insulin and it's not going down. Réjean suspects a kinked canula."

We were in a tough spot, but Réjean's presence reassured me. His daughter is also a type 1 diabetic, so he's highly knowledgeable about all of these things.

After a blood glucose reading of 18.9 mmol/L on his continuous blood glucose monitoring system, Sébastien also thought there might be a malfunction in the pump or with the tubing. If insulin could no longer come through the pump, he would manually inject a dose with a syringe.

At this point, we believed that Sébastien's cognitive faculties were still good enough to make this decision. After all, he had managed his diabetes through several massive endurance challenges over several years. We immediately stopped at the side of the road, and Sébastien decided to inject four units of insulin into his legs, two in each thigh, which is an enormous dose for an athlete expending the level of energy Sébastien was. If his calculation wasn't accurate, we risked a drop in blood sugar to below four mmol/l and ending up with hypoglycemia.

As soon as the injections were done, Sébastien suggested that we take a manual blood glucose reading with a drop of blood. Continuous blood glucose monitoring systems offer many advantages, but traditional blood glucose testing is still the most accurate.

The reading was not 18.9 mmol/L, but rather 14 mmol/L! We realized that we had made a big mistake by injecting four units of insulin. When experiencing unhabitual symptoms, a good practice when managing diabetes is to perform a manual glycemic test before injecting any insulin. But we didn't do that.

Sébastien's continuous glucose monitoring system was defective. With accurate results, we would have administered two units instead of four.

ADAPT OR DIE

Sébastien testing his blood sugar.

We thought we were solving the problem, but we'd created an even bigger one. If Sébastien didn't ingest some sugar, a lot of sugar, actually, the injected insulin would push him into severe hypoglycemia. To top it all off, injecting insulin in the thighs has a much stronger effect during intense exercise.

Sébastien had to get back on the road. Before leaving, he recalibrated the sensor in the hopes of avoiding the same problem later that night. As expected, Sébastien's blood sugar level started to drop rapidly. To combat that, he had a soda and a chocolate bar. Still, his blood sugar continued to drop. Sébastien was well aware of the time bomb in his blood. Without a mega-dose of carbohydrates, a severe hypoglycemic reaction would force him to stop and could be very difficult to manage, with potentially disastrous consequences.

There was still time to stop his blood sugar free fall. Through the communication system, he said: "Prepare me a bottle of sports drink with four scoops of powder." That was 100 grams of carbohydrates, a huge dose. We handed him the bottle through the window of the vehicle, and he gulped it down.

In V1, Réjean blamed himself for not thinking to take a manual reading before giving the injections, but it had all happened so quickly. We pulled over to the side of the road, pulled out the diabetes kit and executed Sébastien's plan without questioning it. It was a moment in the race that reinforced our conviction that we had to manage Sébastien all the time. Despite all his experience and goodwill, fatigue was affecting his decision-making.

We also learned that this high-intensity environment created haste and sped up our decision-making process. Going fast is good, so long as you're going in the right direction. The problem is that mistakes are only discovered after the fact. Thus, it's much better to slow down so that you can clearly think things through and make good decisions.

It was at this point in the race that Philippe introduced the slogan "let's relax." Repeated almost hourly, it was a reminder to slow down to make better decisions. To detach from the intensity and the general stress of the race and think, focus and execute our tasks, big or small.

Unfortunately, even when recalibrated, Sébastien's glucose sensor was still inaccurate to the point that we had to remove it. We no longer had continuous blood glucose reading in V1. This situation persisted for more than 20 hours, until we could insert a new sensor at the trailer. The worst was that Sébastien lost his capacity to monitor his glycemic levels, a nightmare scenario for regulating his nutrition. This curveball added a lot of complexity and was an additional challenge that we, unlike other teams, had to manage. Indeed, even though this was the 40th anniversary of the race, Sébastien would become only the second type 1 diabetic in history to finish the race in the solo category ... if he finished.

In addition to managing the navigation, the nutrition, the communication with the team and driving, we now had to manually test Sébastien's blood sugar. This meant that until his blood sugar could stabilize, we would stop at the side of the road every 15 minutes to prick his finger and take blood sugar readings. What a disadvantage! To add to the complexity, this problem arose during the climbs and descents of Arizona and Colorado. These made the diabetes management even more difficult.

Our first blood glucose reading was pure improvisation. It was about 9 p.m. and night had fallen. Sébastien stopped and put his foot down. We parked V1 next to him and I got out of the vehicle with the diabetes kit, putting it on the hood of the minivan. With fatigue, Sébastien's dexterity had disappeared. He struggled with the small test strip and the lancing pen. He needed light to make the prick. I yelled to Réjean to bring his cellphone to use as a flashlight. With the light, Sébastien pricked his finger, applied pressure to it and soaked the test strip with blood. The reading was 8.9 mmol/L, a much better result!

PERPETUAL ITERATION

The important thing in times of forced adaptation is to react quickly and continually seek to improve the new process through multiple iterations. Sébastien's first blood glucose test was far too slow. However, it was our first attempt, our first step in a new routine. We had to improve if we wanted to remain competitive. The stop had cost us almost four minutes. Four minutes every 15 minutes meant we were losing approximately 16 minutes per hour. We had to improve our routine, and we could do that by optimizing through frequent small iterations.

Back in V1, we asked ourselves the question of how to get that blood glucose stop from four minutes to 30 seconds. We spent the next 15 minutes planning the upcoming stop while continuing to navigate the course and attend to our other tasks. Philippe spoke first: "We need to make the kit easily accessible to Sébastien. Then Réjean added, "I don't think getting out of the car is necessary for the stop. Everything can be done from the passenger window." I was sitting on the passenger side, so it would be me assisting Sébastien. I told Sébastien: "Don't hesitate to tell me what you need during the stop, like a needle, a strip; I can give you the accessories as you need them." Sébastien replied, "Good idea; also, you should have a headlamp so I can see the monitor and where I am pricking my finger."

All these adjustments made a big difference on the second try. We went from four minutes to one minute! Back in the car, we continued to refine the strategy: We changed the positioning of the accessories in the kit and chose strategic sections of the course to stop, like at the tops of the climbs to limit the loss of speed. With each iteration, we gained momentum. We also took advantage of these stops to make water bottle changes that saved some time.

After a few stops, we realized that we really only needed Sébastien for his blood! In the final iterations, I took over the handling of the diabetes kit. Sébastien only had to stop and hold out his finger, and in five seconds I could prick him and apply the precious drop of blood on the test strip. We could communicate the result to Sébastien by radio. From four minutes, we went to 10-second stops.

This notion of iteration is the very foundation of skill development in children, according to Freinet pedagogy. Naturally, a child spontaneously proceeds by an experimental process of trial and error, by trying things out and learning from their mistakes.[*] The Toyota Kata is a similar principle that is also used in many organizations. It is a methodology where a process is continuously repeated, with rapid and incremental improvements each day.[**]

Learning is intimately linked to iteration. In other words, using our knowledge to act and experiment is how we learn. We can then review what we've done and adjust for a better result, then repeat the same process with the new knowledge, learn some more and constantly improve.

THE WAGGLE DANCE

We now needed to pass on what we had learned to the day shift personnel who were coming to take over. We chose to take a few extra minutes during the crew change, even if it meant to stop Sébastien for a little longer, to teach them the basics of our method. Spending a few extra minutes now would save our team time overall.

An interesting fact: Studies have shown that bees communicate by a sort of choreographed movement, the waggle dance. Once the precious nectar flowers are found, the bees return to the hive to inform the rest of the team. Through this bee dance, they can communicate the location of the flowers with impressive accuracy.[***]

---

[*] FREINET, Célestin. *Le tâtonnement expérimental*. Éditions de l'école moderne, 1965.

[**] LANDRY, Sylvain. *Bringing Scientific Thinking to Life: An Introduction to Toyota Kata for Next-Generation Business Leaders (and Those Who Would Like to Be)*. Éditions JFD, 2022.

[***] BIESMEIJER, Jacobus C., and SEELEY, Thomas D. The Use of Waggle Dance Information by Honey Bees Throughout Their Foraging Careers. *Behavioral Ecology and Sociobiology* 2005; vol. 59, no. 1, pp. 133-142.

In this way, bees collaborate and help each other achieve a common goal. Their performance is measured not by individual achievements but by their collective ability to communicate effectively. The principle was the same for the transfer of knowledge in our team. The clearer our communication, the shorter the learning curve would be for the next group, making the whole team more efficient.

The efforts paid off, and everything went well for the day shift. The more the day progressed, the more their comfort level grew. After countless iterations, that great disadvantage of diabetes became a new opportunity. We could cool Sébastien down more frequently with our portable pump shower and replace his water bottles more regularly. We also combined our diabetes and nutrition stops into one. Once Sébastien's blood sugar stabilized, we reduced the frequency of blood sugar tests to two per hour.

When we arrived in Cortez, Colorado, where the RV team was waiting for us, Manon installed a new continuous glucose monitoring sensor on Sébastien. After confirming that the new device was working properly, we were all relieved to be able to get real-time blood sugar readings. During this crisis, we were able to limit the damage and lose only two positions in the ranking.

AN ENERGY-FILLED WELCOME

Leaving La Veta on day 5, we entered the second half of the race feeling optimistic despite the challenges diabetes had presented. Other teams certainly faced their own challenges, and at least a dozen of them had dropped out so far.

The next stop was in the state of Kansas, which is known for its flat terrain and high winds. Unfortunately, a heat wave hit the plains just as we passed through. The temperature was almost as hot as in the desert, approaching 40 degrees Celsius. The heat wave brought a hot wind out of the south. Sébastien, crossing the plains of Kansas from west to east, had a side wind.

While some competitors thrive on mountainous conditions, Sébastien excels on flat and windy terrain. Jokingly, we often said that Sébastien was an old diesel tractor: it takes a while to warm up, but once it's going,

BUILDING UNSTOPPABLE TEAMS

2022 RAAM Solo Male (under 50)

Country	Current Rank	Entry	Time Station	Distance Travelled (in miles)	Average Speed (in miles per hour)	Status
	1	455 Svata Bozak	26	1543.21	12.89	
	2	659 Simon Potter	25	1511.10	12.09	
	3	658 Phil Fox	24	1444.90	12.07	
	4	610 Rachid Rachure	24	1444.90	12.01	
	5	599 Christian Mauduit	24	1444.90	11.74	
	6	661 Sébastien Sasseville	23	1395.00	11.73	
	7	627 Graham Macken	21	1272.20	10.29	
	8	624 Bharay Pannu	21	1272.20	10.18	
	9	671 Arvis Sprude	20	1200.90	10.33	
	0	645 Rainer Steinberger	17	1030.70	14.90	DNF
	0	655 Martin Neitzke	9	602.90	13.76	DNF

On day 5, Sébastien was in 12th place overall and sixth place in the under 50 category.

there's no stopping it. The plains of Kansas were an advantageous terrain for Sébastien, but we were also aware that he had burned a lot of matches to get over the mountains over the last three days, as he is simply not the greatest of climbers.

Our chances of a podium finish in his age category were still very real, especially with the course profile looking flat for the next 1,500 kilometers. On day 5, Sébastien covered 416 kilometers. We were all impressed to see how good his morale remained. He was tired, of course, but kept smiling at all the refueling stops. His energy was contagious and drove the team to surpass itself despite the fatigue that was setting in.

For the fifth Seb to Bed, we stopped at the 23rd time station in the town of Ulysses, Kansas. We were welcomed like kings by an army of volunteers. To our great surprise, we even saw a Canadian flag! All the volunteers encouraged Sébastien as he passed by. Because of the flag, Philippe even confused them for our team. What a boost of energy! These small gestures made the difference for the last pedal strokes of the day.

Of the 54 time stations of RAAM, eight were staffed by volunteers. These time stations were usually located in community centers or schools. They included volunteer-prepared snacks, bathrooms with showers, rest areas and screens to watch the race live. With weather this hot, the icing on the cake was obviously air conditioning!

THE RV LEAKS

While Sébastien was sleeping, I took the opportunity to go around the team to see how everyone was doing. Orphé gave me some bad news. He had just noticed that the RV was losing oil. Orphé had great mechanical knowledge and reassured me that the situation was under control . . . for now. He could buy us some time by filling the oil tank to get to the next stop. However, we would have to find a solution soon as a leak could damage the engine. After diabetes, another weight had landed on our shoulders!

The next day, I was in the RV with Orphé when we realized the extent of the problem. We were losing much more oil than we thought. The RV needed four liters of oil to make it through day 6. That day, Orphé tried for several hours to fix the leak as best he could. But with few tools at his disposal, he was unsuccessful.

I sat down with Orphé to evaluate our options. Complicating the issue was that we had rented the RV directly from its owner, back in Canada. The first option was to continue to buy time by filling the oil tank. However, this strategy risked damaging the engine over the course of the thousands of kilometers we had left, with no guarantee that the situation would not get worse. The second option was to find a garage to repair the oil leak. The third option, if no garage could fix it, was to leave the trailer behind and rent another vehicle to complete the race.

We concluded that the second option was best. However, we were still driving through rural areas, and garages were rare. Moreover, as it was a Sunday, most of them were closed. Orphé noted that we would be passing through St. Louis, Missouri, on day 8. This was a good lead.

After countless calls, Orphé finally managed to find a garage. The mechanic was a Good Samaritan: although he specialized in trucks and didn't usually repair RVs, he was confident he could help us. With the travel and repair time, the team would be without the RV for a minimum of 48 hours.

PROTECTING THE EXPERIENCE

In this situation, we instructed the entire team to not tell Sébastien about the problem. We didn't want mechanical concerns to become a source of worry or distraction for him. All his remaining energy had to be channeled into his one and only task: pedaling. But how were we going to hide the absence of the RV for more than 48 hours from Sébastien? It became a game!

We brainstormed to develop a strategy. The goal was to ensure that this glitch had no impact on Sébastien's experience and performance. Like the customer experience in a business, no matter what issues are present internally, the objective is always to offer a frictionless experience to the customer. Providing exceptional service to our athlete became our motivation for the next 48 hours.

This obstacle brought the team closer together. Nothing like a little bit of adversity to build engagement and bond a group. Our ultimate goal remained the same, but with the added challenges of one less vehicle and fewer teammates. The seventh Seb to Bed marked a farewell to Manon and Orphé, who left with the RV. During the evening, we reorganized the luggage, and Manon took advantage of the RV's kitchen to plan the next day's meals. A team of eight people remained to support Sébastien with the two minivans. All occupants of the minivans had to take enough of their personal belongings to last a minimum of 48 hours. Also, all the performance equipment, such as the physiotherapy table, the plastic boxes containing the equipment required for Seb to Bed and Seb to Bike and all tools, had to be transferred to the minivans.

There was no guarantee that Manon and Orphé would be back with the team before the end of the race. If the garage detected a more serious problem than expected, it was possible that we would only see them again at the finish line. For the next 48 hours, all our attention was on Sébastien and we almost forgot about the RV. Sébastien maintained his

12th position, and to my surprise, I received a call on day 9 informing me that the repair was complete. At around 8:30 p.m. during the ninth Seb to Bed, Manon and Orphé rejoined us.

This ordeal is a great example of the power of an autonomous team. We solved problems without requiring the input of the whole team. To create such empowerment, there were two important and necessary steps.

First, everyone was given roles consistent with their area of genius and skills. Orphé is a good example. He absolutely loves fixing cars. From start to finish, he took ownership of the problem and led the efforts to resolve it, enabling me to keep my full attention on my own responsibilities.

Second, the expectations concerning such events had been clearly communicated by Sébastien. Before the race, he made it clear that he didn't want to be informed of operational problems so he could concentrate fully on the race. He gave us full autonomy in all our decisions. Then, a lot of time and energy was dedicated to building a team of experts. Sébastien trusted us. We took his trust seriously.

Now, trust isn't an expectation of perfection. Trust should be comforting, not stressful! Sébastien trusted our skills, our intelligence and our good judgment. He believed that we would do the best we could. Consequently, we felt supported and safe. His assumption of best effort and best intention in the team led to a more engaged and highly empowered group that in the end was able to weather the storm.

CHAPTER 14

HITTING THE WALL

Sébastien Sasseville

From this point on in the race, many things are hazy to me. I'll share what I recall experiencing up to day 9, and in the next chapter you'll get Gabriel's take on what transpired.

Many RAAM veterans say that the race really starts at the halfway point. In endurance racing, it's what you do now that dictates how you will perform five or 10 hours later. Early mistakes are always exposed later. RAAM (and business) is no different. It's what you do during the first half of the race that determines if, and in what manner, you'll get to the finish line.

We were now in Missouri. I had covered about 3,500 of the 4,800 kilometers of the race and was in 12th place overall.

It was an excellent ranking, right in line with my expectations. Just outside the top 10, but certainly a great achievement considering it was my first participation in the most difficult ultra-cycling race in the world.

Regarding fatigue, I was right on the edge. So long as I could get two hours' sleep during the breaks, I found the energy to display a good performance for the following 24 hours. At this point, it was the team that kept me moving forward.

Cognitively, I could focus only on pushing the bike. Any other considerations, even minor ones, were beyond my capacity. Thinking about logistics was totally out of the question. I was vulnerable, but I felt

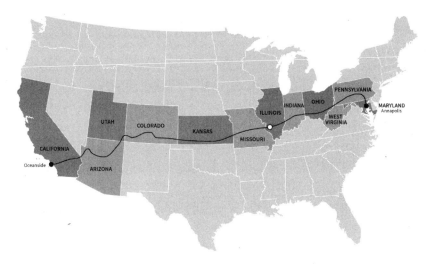

An overview of the road traveled by day 9.

supported. I felt confident, as every team member was giving everything they had and some more. I was bathed in goodwill and kindness, which allowed me to focus on the bike and nothing else.

NOTICE AND ACKNOWLEDGE

A high-performance team must be able to identify threats so they can quickly develop the appropriate response. Regardless of the context, accidents rarely happen without some sort of warning. Either a threat goes unrecognized (fail to notice), or it is identified but not responded to quickly enough with the necessary force (fail to acknowledge). Ignoring small threats is dangerous because they then grow. And it's always easier to deal with a tinier menace; killing a fly is much easier than killing a bear.

By day 8 I was in a great position, but things were unfortunately about to go south. During that day, I was more or less aware that I was participating in RAAM. I was hovering between a dream and reality, certainly in an altered state of consciousness. All day I thought I was riding with friends. In fact, I often wondered where they were and why I was alone. I didn't really know where I was, but I wasn't that bothered and kept moving forward without question, much like one does in a dream. I had forgotten that I was sleeping in the RV or a motel. In my head, the plan was to meet my friends at a campground around suppertime to share a meal.

Interestingly, my mind began to clear during the last hour before reaching the next resting point, when I was most physically stressed. It was as if the pain had woken me up and brought me back to reality. I realized that I had spent a good part of the day in a delirium, which was somewhat disturbing. I shared a watered-down version of what had happened with the team. I didn't want to alarm them, and I certainly didn't want to be slowed down or forced to extend my sleep. The first mistake: I failed to notice how bad things were. I also did not share all the information I had with the team.

Rather than being alarmed, the team didn't give enough importance to what I had just experienced. In fact, it had been expected. I was in a state of fatigue that very few people will experience in their lives; given this, it was not a surprise to anyone that I had been day dreaming. The second mistake: they failed to acknowledge how bad things were.

Clearly something was wrong. There were signals, but we ignored them.

There are usually warning signs of potential dangers. The 1986 Space Shuttle Challenger disaster is a good example of an ignored risk. The cause of the accident was attributed to a failure in a seal. The decision-makers had all the necessary data documenting a decrease in seal performance at cold temperatures. They were blinded by a desire for performance, paralyzed by political considerations. The accident could have been prevented if they had taken the risk more seriously.[*]

As with the shuttle, we ignored the threat before us.

I was given a couple of hours of sleep, and off I went. But there was something lurking behind the scenes: the lack of sleep of the first three days had created a ticking time bomb.

An extreme fortitude is a double-edged sword, and it can turn against the athlete. When the body gives up but the mind wants to keep going, it creates a potentially perilous situation. But no matter how strong the will, the body always has the last word.

---

[*] UPI. Key Portions of Commission Report on Challenger Accident. *New York Times*. 10 June 1986.

THE BEGINNING OF HALLUCINATIONS

There is a lot of literature on the best sleep strategies for RAAM. While it all concludes by stating that the best strategy is the one that works for you, some trends emerge. Studies show that a lack of sleep early in the race will always result in major struggles later in the race.[*]

I had already been hallucinating at night for a few days. This part didn't bother me too much. To be honest, I enjoyed it. Most RAAM participants report hallucinating. For me, it didn't entail a loss of control or total disconnection from reality. Rather, the hallucinations were visual in nature: trees, plants, mailboxes and other things on the side of the road turned into faces, strange objects or cartoonish pictures.

What I saw was always dark, black and a bit evil. I remember a black veil floating in front of me, diabolical creatures that quietly came out of the pits to become plants again when I rode by them. All this could be scary at times, but I was able to remember that none of it was real, and that there was no danger. Sometimes, with extreme fatigue, the human mind naturally goes to bad thoughts when it has too much time to think. That, coupled with evil visions . . . it's easy to lose your mind.

But I enjoyed these visions very much. I'm not a very creative person, so I was fascinated by what my brain could create. The show was unfolding before me, I couldn't control it and I constantly switched between fright and wonder. The less I tried to stop or control the hallucinations, the more they intensified and the more I enjoyed them.

Moments of clarity punctuated these times. I realized that I was pushing the body and mind to a place where few people are willing to go, and that I was having a unique experience. We exchange pain for experiences that are otherwise difficult to access. For many people, the hallucinations, the extreme sleep deprivation, not to mention the 400 to 500 kilometers of cycling per day, would be torture.

I'm not saying it's easy, but truth be told, I never feel more alive than during these hallucinations, or more specifically, during the moments of lucidity that intersperse them.

---

[*] GRUEBELE, Martin, and SCOTT, Gregory. *Masters RAAM: A Winning Strategy*. HB Publications, 2016.

If you pay attention, you realize that you are having an experience that so very few people on earth will ever have. Therefore, you are also granted access to lessons that are just as unique and rare.

So you become thankful for those moments. Thankful for adversity. You appreciate that this instant is in fact an exchange. That if you want to gain something extraordinary, you need to provide an extraordinary effort.

Nothing will make you feel more positive than doing hard things. Nothing is more beautiful than a human in a state of maximal effort. As my favorite quote says, "Happiness is in freely consented effort."

GOING TO WAR

There were only 1,200 kilometers to go. It was 10 p.m., night had already fallen, and I was chatting with the team on our communication system while riding. I was in a state of extreme fatigue, but all in all still functional and moving forward smoothly. No delirium, and I was fully aware that I was in a race. To tell you the truth, I felt great, and the team in V1 was also in great spirits.

We discussed the last few days, the strategy and our options. We were in a very good position in the ranking. A finish under the day 11 mark was not impossible. Two thousand twenty-two was one of the hottest years in the history of RAAM, so times were a little slower than usual.

Basically, we had two choices. One, continue to the finish line on autopilot with the same strategy and be conservative. Cycles of 21 or 22 hours straight on the bike every day, a two-hour sleep period, with quick transitions to bed and back to the bike. This "guaranteed" us to finish within the 12-day limit and place very well.

Or . . . go all in and try to finish as high in the standings as possible. This roll of the dice meant eliminating two-hour rest periods and instead taking 30-minute naps as needed, probably two or three a day. The naps would be taken in V1, dressed in bike gear, shoes on feet, helmet on head. This would eliminate the logistics and time required for Seb to Bed and Seb to Bike. It would give us a savings of at least 90 minutes per day.

This scenario meant reshuffling the team and shifts. In short, changing everything for the last three days. Marie-Michèle would have to sit in

V1 for most of the shifts. We felt it was crucial to always have her expertise as a physiotherapist available to get me back on my feet if needed. Philippe, a beast, had already spent 100 percent of the race in V1, and he planned to stay there until the end.

The second option was a gamble. High risk, high reward. It was risky, because we knew that if things went wrong, there was a chance we wouldn't finish. But the potential reward was commensurate with the risk. A top 10 or even a top five finish would be out of this world for a first-time RAAM participant. What to do?

I was aware that this was my last big project for a few years. I knew that I wanted to take a break from racing after RAAM, and I wanted to finish strong. I also knew that I tend to lean too much towards the slow-and-steady endurance approach rather than the combative one. During my preparation for RAAM, I worked on this aspect in my mental preparation to develop a more competitive spirit. So here I was, with an opportunity to show that I could be a fighter until the last moment.

As a team, after weighing the pros and cons at length, we decided to go for it. Around 2 a.m. on day 7, we said to ourselves: "Let's go to war. It's do or die."

Philippe and Gabriel turned off the radio to begin planning for the last few days and to communicate the change in strategy and its impact to the rest of the team. I continued to pedal silently in the light projected by V1. After the few days of adjustment at the beginning of the race, I was in familiar territory for several days. Although in hindsight there was nothing normal about what I was doing, I was used to it and knew what I had to do every day. Now, I was back in a situation full of uncertainty. With the decision we had just made, it was a return to the feeling at the starting line: a mixture of excitement and fear.

THE HOUSE OF CARDS COLLAPSES

It's difficult to make a judgment about what happened next, after the fact, when you have a clear head and all the data. Even to this day, I don't feel like we made a bad decision. We went with the data we had, and we were ambitious. All in all, thanks to this new strategy I rode 483 kilometers from day 7 to day 8, my second-best day of RAAM. Our new ambitious plan also made me gain a few places in the standings. At one point we were in ninth place overall.

However, this slight increase in pace was followed by a total collapse. Because of my sleep debt from the first few days, I didn't have enough energy to sustain such a pace. Like a house of cards, I was fragile, and it didn't take a big gust of wind — in our case, all it took was a change in strategy — to collapse the structure. In the hours following our decision to go for it, I expended too much energy in the moments when I needed to rest — for example, during the descents and when I had tailwinds.

On the morning of day 9, I was drained. I had a very difficult sequence between four and seven in the morning. I was completely flat and to makes things worse, we were in a very hilly area; I was moving very, very slowly. The team did everything to motivate me, but nothing was working. Psychologically, it was very difficult because I felt my body falling apart. I was passed by a few cyclists and had an inkling of what was unfolding — that things could, and would, get ugly.

At around 7 a.m. the whole team gathered for a change of personnel in V1. I was in the worst physical and psychological state of the race. I was emotional, fragile, absent, withdrawn, completely silent, looking down. I had tears in my eyes, but I wasn't just sad. I was angry. Angry that I was so broken, angry that I couldn't sprint to the finish line. I felt like I was letting the team down and not measuring up.

I couldn't admit that I was falling apart and that I had reached a limit. Or rather, I had reached a limit and wasn't satisfied. For the first time, I felt a fair amount of concern among the team. They had never seen me like this. From the beginning, I wasn't in operations, but it was critical for me to provide a clear vision, to be inspiring and inspired, and to make sure that everyone on the team felt like we were doing something important. That morning, I was not in that spirit in any way.

Today, we talk a lot about vulnerability in our organizations. We want leaders who are human, humble, authentic and vulnerable. The question is, how can I, as a leader, be strong in my vulnerability? How can a leader's vulnerability become a motivating factor for his troops?

I have a few ideas. Of course, each leader will have his or her own recipe, and there's no instruction manual for vulnerability.

HITTING THE WALL

At this junction in the race, I experienced a loss of control. Leaders often love control. To be clear, I'm not talking about control in any negative sense. I am referring to the hundreds of hours of training an athlete does before a competition to be in control when the time comes to perform. Controlling one's destiny simply means creating favorable circumstances by preparing rigorously before an important event.

The fact is that we cannot control everything. The strength in vulnerability is determined not by our degree of control but rather by our response to our loss of it. We must be able to ask for help, stay true to the vision and stay aligned with our values, especially during turbulence.

What can be even harder than asking for help is receiving help. So many times in our lives, we need help, help is offered, and our response is something like, "I'm fine." Twenty hands were about to reach to me, and accepting their help would be salutary to our mission.

Being vulnerable also means being present to oneself and others without having to filter your emotions, the difficulties you're undergoing and joys you experience — indeed, without victimizing yourself or flaunting your happiness before others. In practical terms in the workplace, this might mean not hiding your difficulties and at the same time staying the course with bravery and resilience.

I also believe that people are inspired by vulnerability if it emerges from total and complete effort. It can inspire one's team when one comes up against a real limit after having pushed many times beyond what one initially thought possible.

For eight days I had been sleeping two hours a day, sometimes less. We had climbed to ninth place among the world's best, while more than 50 percent of the participants had dropped out. There was no doubt that I had left everything on the course and was giving my best effort.

My condition at the 7 a.m. exchange point on day 9 warranted an extended stop. Marie-Michèle checked me over, and I slept for 30 minutes. As planned, I slept in V1 in the front passenger seat. What luxury. With the short time to fall asleep, not to mention the ambient noise of the parking lot where we were, those minutes passed quickly and were far from being the most restorative. As with every nap in V1, the team would wake me up as abruptly as possible by opening the door of the vehicle quickly. It was a bit cruel, but necessary. It was always a shock.

My arms would instantly stiffen, as if I were instinctively putting myself in a defensive position for a split second. This was followed by the realization that I had to get back on the bike, a little dejected and with pain in my legs and buttocks. Without making a chapter out of it, the pain in the buttocks was often the main limiting factor. Imagine an open wound that burns with every pedal stroke.

I have little recollection of the beginning of day 9. In the next chapter, Gabriel will discuss at length the day that changed everything. I certainly had a different experience from him and the rest of the team. The first few hours were uneventful, but I lost my connection to reality once again. I was daydreaming on the bike; I have a memory of seeing local cyclists on a bike path across the street and thinking they were stray RAAM cyclists. Or was it me who was on the wrong trail? The more hours that passed, the more I lost touch with reality. My mind was slowly slipping.

My body also quietly powered down. My average speed slowed from under 20 km/h, then to under 15 km/h, not far from standing still. Yet my legs were burning like I was sprinting. Legs burning at the slightest effort is a sign that the body is preparing to shut down. The body struggles to get a moment of rest; if it doesn't get it, it eventually stops moving. As I said earlier, the body always has the last word.

I was now dreaming that I was lost, again only partially aware that I was participating in RAAM. I couldn't see V1 behind me, so I stopped. Standing with the bike still between my legs, I laid my upper body and head on the handlebars of my bike. A team member startled me — I had fallen asleep in that position and was about to fall over. In fact, there were two: Philippe and Martin, but I don't really remember anything more about it.

They asked me how I was doing; I asked if I was on the right path. They tried to motivate me and wake me up. When I started out, I was going less than 10 km/h, and eventually I couldn't pedal anymore. The team stopped me a few kilometers further on. My speed was much too slow. At this point, psychologically, I was in free fall. I fell apart.

The day before, I had almost gotten hit. In 20 years of cycling, this was the moment when I was most afraid. The car grazed me. I even heard a scream from inside the car. A second car had passed very close to me a few hours later. On the morning of day 9, I made a false move, 100

HITTING THE WALL

percent related to fatigue, where I suddenly ended up in the middle of the road. The traffic was very heavy; cars were driving at 70 km/h, and it was a miracle that I didn't get hit.

I was in tears, unable to pedal, with a strong feeling that I had to get off these roads or else a tragedy would occur. I felt like I was one pedal stroke away from a heart attack. I told Philippe that it was over for me, that I was ready to throw in the towel. I told him that it was the end of our RAAM.

Philippe looked at me and then told me: "Sébastien, this is an unacceptable attitude, we're not stopping."

I'm not going to lie; I was a little upset! But it was at that point and in the hours that followed that the team saved our race.

God knows that this episode was one of the darkest times of my sporting career. Ironically, today, it's one of my best memories, and certainly also a moment that led to one of the most valuable lessons of our RAAM.

Given my condition over the last few hours, several discussions about potential adjustments were already underway. The team had found the next available hotel on the road, about 45 kilometers from my position. An easy coffee shop ride in normal circumstances, but at 15 km/h, it was going to be three hours of hard work.

This was our race, and they weren't ready to give up. They were a well-rested team of 10 smart and driven individuals, in full control, doing the all the necessary calculations and analysis to get us to the finish line. I was asked to continue, and 10 people would support me.

The bottom of the barrel on day 9.

Getting to that hotel was difficult. At the beginning, I was riding at 12 km/h, and I stopped every two kilometers. Halfway through, I took a 15-minute nap, and slowly my speed improved. Around 3:30 p.m. we arrived at the hotel so that I could lie down and the team could reformulate the plan.

NO EGO

There is a lot to be said about the last 48 hours. First, the decision to change the plan. I am comfortable with the idea of wanting to be combative, to change the plan and take risks. In life, it's important to take risks, even if you sometimes make mistakes or fail. My uneasiness with this decision is rather that it was anchored in the ego.

By choosing to aim for a result, we moved away from our mission of having an impact. With a DNF (did not finish), we wouldn't have fulfilled our mission. In retrospect, the risk was not worth it. The top three positions were out of our reach. We were in ninth place, and the chances of catching up to those in front were very slim. We had everything to lose and little to gain.

Finishing RAAM is an incredible achievement. Today, more people summit Mount Everest in a year than have finished RAAM in its 40 years of existence. The finish line, regardless of ranking, was going to be a message of hope and inspiration for everyone living with type 1 diabetes.

Sometimes a bird in the hand is better than two in the bush. Our decision was not motivated by the right reasons. We should have acted more wisely, finishing the RAAM in the top 10, which for a first participation would have been extraordinary. We had already optimized our logistics, and the team was in full control. We should have remembered that we were rookies, recognized that we were among the best rookies, been proud of that, and finished strong. Instead, we wanted more and were willing to risk everything.

DANGER OR DISCOMFORT?

Having said that, despite the near misses on the bike and my feeling of having to leave the road, I must state that the team made the right decision to keep me on the saddle. During my years of mountaineering, we always asked one question: are we currently facing danger or discomfort?

In high altitude, when we face a danger, we must stop, take a few steps back, and return with more expertise, different tools, or simply when the weather is more favorable.

In a professional context, this translates to a new process, technological changes or a restructuring of the team — more often than not, these are discomforts, not dangers. In the face of discomfort, big or small, you must keep moving forward, be resilient and simply be open to challenges that may lie ahead.

The trap to avoid is reacting to discomfort as if it were danger. Yes, it had been a close call with the cars, but thank God nothing happened. There was no longer any real threat. And with a little more sleep, I could limit the possibility of such mishaps.

THE POWER OF THE TEAM

If our adventure had stopped with a DNF, this book wouldn't exist. No one wants to read or hear the story of a DNF. Of course, on a personal level, you learn and grow a lot with a DNF. These lessons are extremely valuable, and sometimes even more powerful than what we learn from a win.

But more often we like to hear about results and success. You bought this book to boost your and/or your team's performance, probably saying to yourself that there should be a good tip or two in there. Even when we read about failure, we do so to learn from it; we love stories of failure with heroes and heroines who get back up to fight on. Aware of all this, Gabriel and I knew we had to finish this race.

What the team did for me and for us on day 9 was extraordinary. It illustrated not only the importance of surrounding yourself with good people, but more specifically, trusting those astonishingly reliable and competent people to make important decisions when you are unable to do so yourself.

It must be said that there was a lot more love than you think in Philippe's comment that "this is an unacceptable attitude." In my opinion, there are two key lessons to extract from his message. First, Philippe did not want to allow doubt to insert itself in our heads. When you start considering failure as an option, the next thing your brain will do is rationalize it and find good reasons to justify it. Your brain will make the failure seem not as bad. In short, we're looking for excuses, sometimes very good ones, to make the loss hurt a little less.

Second, in a team, some individuals embody one of the team's or company's values a little more than others. Our three core values were collaboration, performance and adaptation. Philippe embodied performance more than anyone in the team. The right person, in the right chair, at the right time. The situation demanded our performance value to be embodied to the maximum, and no one other than Philippe could have done it so remarkably.

I often jokingly say that if at that moment I had asked Manon, our oldest team member, and let's be frank, the team's mom, whether I could stop, she would have told me something like, "Sébastien, we love you so much, you are so amazing, if you want to stop, that's no problem! We're so proud of you already. And this race is insane anyway! If you want to stop, that's totally okay."

The right person, in the right chair, at the right time.

As I mentioned in chapter 10, resilience is a muscle. It is developed and strengthened through training. But like muscles, resilience can get tired. After a really intense workout, your muscles need to recuperate. They haven't disappeared, but while in recovery they're much less strong.

By day 9, after all of the incredibly intense efforts I'd made, my resilience was exhausted. I got down on my knees and wanted to give up. It was because of my trusted teammates, who were able to make a better decision than I, that our race continued. Of all the things they did for me, this is what I will always remember most.

A PREMONITORY MEETING

If I may, I'd like to take you back to June 11, three days before the start of the race. The team had arrived in California that morning, our excitement at its peak.

Sometimes life smiles upon you. Better than that, life makes sure to whisper in your ears what you need to hear. The universe makes sure that out of the eight billion humans walking the earth, the two individuals who need to share something meet "by chance."

In the evening, we went to a long boardwalk along the Pacific Ocean to take team pictures. The place was crowded, and we were all wearing our team T-shirts, cleverly designed by Marc-Antoine. We were easily recognizable, and our participation in RAAM clearly displayed. A passerby also stood out with his long, curly hair dyed blue, red and white. This character was Jim Trout.

On seeing him we all had the same thought: he's a weirdo. Jim walked up to us and asked if we were participating in RAAM, and if we were participating as a team or in the solo category.

It turned out that Jim was also a participant in the solo category. In talking with him, we quickly realized that despite his eccentricity, he was a very wise man. Jim is in his fifties, his day job is as a pharmacist, and this was his third time participating in RAAM. He had managed to finish the event once but was forced to drop out on his second attempt. His support team consisted of his two teenage children, his spouse, friends and some family members. His stripe of red hair was in the center. For every 1,000 miles (1,600 kilometers), or one-third of the race, he would shave his head on one side, with the goal of finishing the race with a red mohawk. He simply told us that it was to spice up the race, and that a red mohawk was cool.

Given his experience, we asked him several questions. Among others, I asked him what was the best advice he had to offer a rookie like me, what was his most valuable learning experience and what were the most important mistakes to avoid.

I didn't know it yet, but Jim's answer would serve me well on day 9.

"Your body will give out. Be ready for it. It's inevitable, it's going to happen, that's RAAM. It happens to all participants, without exception. You're going to be frustrated with your body, you're going to wonder why you can't move forward. You're going to feel like you're letting your team down. You're not. When that happens, welcome that moment, don't try to fight it. At that point, frustration makes us tend to lash out, when the body needs the opposite in order to start moving forward again. When your body falls apart, slow down, stop and take care of it."

On day 9, I thought a lot about what Jim had told me. I certainly couldn't avoid the feelings of anger and frustration. There was also plenty of self-flagellation, as if I was forgetting that I had just cycled 22 hours a day, nine days in a row; as if the collapse was happening for no good reason. But little by little, the echo of Jim's wise and kind words took hold of me.

THE BREAKING POINT

There is something beautiful in meeting breaking points. They are limits that we have reached. Clearly defined and exposed, they are almost quantifiable. After all, don't we do these things to discover and push our limits? What good is it if we don't find them?

If you decide to run a marathon to test your limits, have you really pushed your limit if you finish the marathon? For a million dollars, could you have run an extra mile? Five? Most likely. Finding your breaking point is about hitting a real limit. It's persevering to the point of failure to find out what you are capable of. To seek your breaking point is to have the courage to plan your defeat.

I like to set the bar very high so that I can come up against my limits. A face-to-face with myself, a very intimate and revealing encounter. The good news is that breaking points are not fixed. To really push our limits and accomplish the extraordinary, we must really know, experience and understand our limits. Only in this way can we craft a strategy to surpass it.

Jim finished the race in fourth place.

CHAPTER 15

MAKING DECISIONS IN UNCERTAIN TIMES

Gabriel Renaud

I never doubted our ability to finish RAAM. During the six months of preparation and the first nine days of the race, I was full of optimism. With a seasoned endurance athlete like Sébastien and a team that was so ready and determined, failing never crossed my mind. All the team members shared this optimism. However, when Sébastien reached his breaking point, that optimism was definitely shaken.

Let's rewind the tape by just a few hours and allow me to tell the story of the morning of day 9 from my perspective. When I saw Sébastien arrive at time station 39 in Bloomington, Indiana, I must admit that, for the first time, I had doubts. Several thoughts crossed my mind. Had all the preparation work been in vain? Was the story worth telling if we didn't finish? Had Sébastien's physical preparation been adequate?

That morning should have been a celebration for Sébastien. He arrived at a staffed time station, where volunteers and our entire team were there to greet him. It was a beautiful sunny day, not as hot as the previous days. This stop also marked a change of team in V1. All the elements were there to give a good boost of energy to Sébastien, who adored the rare moments when the whole team was gathered.

When I saw Sébastien, his physical condition affected me greatly. He was destroyed. His eyes were glassy, his usual smile was absent and the skin on his face was hanging off. All of his enthusiasm was gone, and I thought to myself, "He's not having fun anymore." I thought maybe it was just a dark cloud that would pass. Unfortunately, later in the day, I realized that my concerns were well founded. Sébastien had hit the wall. He'd reached his breaking point, the inevitable destiny that Jim Trout had described before the race. The decision to abandon the two-hour rest periods had cost him, and us, dearly. The short naps on the side of the road had not been enough of a recharge, and he was completely drained.

I discussed the situation with Philippe while Sébastien slept for 30 minutes. We had to adjust the strategy again. Sébastien was at the end of his rope; he simply had to sleep, otherwise the risk of a DNF was real. Philippe told me that his goal for the day was to get him as far as possible, but to plan a Seb to Bed earlier in the day than usual. A few minutes later, when Sébastien woke up and the V1 team left with him. I left with Dan, Marc-Antoine and Valérie in V2 to go buy a part for the bike.

On the way to the store, we started to list and analyze what our best options would be to get Sébastien to the finish line. This was the moment when we all realized how little room we had to maneuver. We projected our arrival time in Annapolis based on Sébastien's average speed. For the first time, we discussed the odds of not finishing the race. We considered all the possible hypotheses to resurrect Sébastien. A pivotal decision was coming — one that would be crucial to our ability to cross the finish line.

ELEVATE ABOVE THE CLOUDS

Until day 8, I was in V1 every day either for the day or night shift. On day 9, I decided to make way for those who had less opportunity to accompany Sébastien in V1. The timing for this could not have been better.

When you are in V1, there is always something to do or think about. If you're not serving Sébastien, you're planning the next stop. I'm energized by that type of highly solicited environment, but it's not always conducive to making the best strategic decisions. The hectic pace of the daily operations doesn't leave time to step back and take a high-level view so as to analyze all the options, like the eagle described in chapter 2.

Up until now in RAAM, I was often in the frenzy of operations and sometimes lost sight of the grand scheme. I had to elevate above the clouds to see the big picture and to make better decisions.

UP AGAINST THE WALL

In V2 I was able to take the time to analyze all our options. I could also take advantage of the experience of Dan and Marc-Antoine, who had been part of the ride across Canada with Sébastien the year before. They shared with me their perspective on Sébastien's current condition. They confirmed that never during the Canada crossing had Sébastien been in such a pitiful state. I immediately pulled out a sheet of paper, and we began to make a list of possible scenarios. After a process of elimination, we had two final options.

Option 1: Go back to Sébastien's original sleep schedule. This was the strategy of the first eight days: sleeping two to three hours in a row per "night." This strategy gave us a larger buffer at the finish. However, it did not allow us to resurrect Sébastien. This strategy put us at the finish line approximately five hours before the final cut-off.

Option 2: Do what we called a Seb to Super Bed. This strategy involved a six-hour stop, which we dubbed the *reset*. The reset gave Sébastien a "solid" five hours of sleep. Then, for the following nights, we would also revert to the initial sleep strategy. This option allowed us to (potentially) get Sébastien back up in the best possible shape, but it also meant that we would be at the finish line an hour before the final cut-off.

The ultimate question was: to do a reset or not? On the sheet of paper, I projected how fast Sébastien would have to cycle to make the cut-off. For option 1, Sébastien had to maintain an average of 16 km/h. For option 2, Sébastien had to maintain an average of 17.3 km/h. This was a relatively attainable speed for Sébastien, considering that his speed between the last six time stations had been 19.5 km/h. Note that these average speeds include all breaks and the time when Sébastien is not moving.

With this data, the decision to go with option two was obvious. In fact, we had no choice. It was either that, or Sébastien might not finish the race. We couldn't attack the climbs and descents of the Appalachians

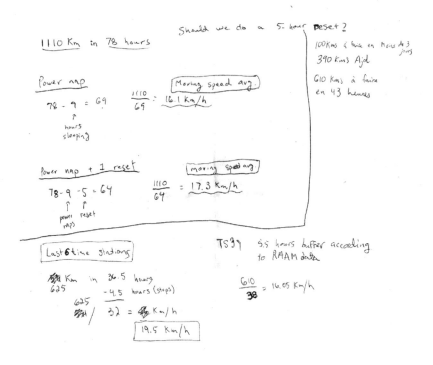

The original sheet of our calculations. Option 1 is identified *power nap* and option 2 is the *Seb to bed + 1 reset*. On the top left, there are 1,110 km to go in 78 hours. Bottom left, Sébastien's speed over the last six time stations. At the top right, the ultimate question: *to do a reset or not?*

without him getting some sleep. But there was one caveat: this decision did not offer any leeway, and the whole team had to be aware of this. Now we had to present the plan to the VI team to get a consensus — especially from Philippe, who would have an important voice in this decision.

I called VI and told them I wanted to talk as soon as possible, on the shoulder of the road if necessary. By this time, it was about 9 a.m. VI had already been with Sébastien on the road for an hour, so we went to join them.

Once we got together, I explained my calculations to Philippe. Philippe, an intuitive guy, didn't hesitate for a second and said, "Let's go with option 2." It was gratifying that we were all on the same page. Then, I asked him his opinion on how many kilometers Sébastien could still ride today. He replied, "The last hour was good, but he could come apart anytime; let's aim for 75 to 100 kilometers to finish the day."

DARE TO HAVE FUN

We gathered the entire team to share the updated plan. I shared the strategy of doing a five-hour Seb to Super Bed at the end of the day. I explained why this decision was risky. Our estimated arrival time was about an hour from cut-off, providing no leeway for any contingencies. I asked everyone to eliminate all non-value-added actions. Once I explained the strategy and everyone was on board, Philippe took his turn: "We have a job to do, but from now on, we are no longer in podium mode, we are in fun mode. I want us to organize a party for Sébastien."

Philippe was so right! At this point, a podium was unrealistic; Sébastien had accumulated too much of a deficit on the leading athletes. It was by having fun that he could finish the race. Fun is what motivates and brings people together. It is well documented that when we are enjoying something and laughing, we secrete hormones such as serotonin and dopamine that increase energy levels.[*]

Philippe went back to the fundamental reason why we had all joined this team: to have an unforgettable experience together. We had to help Sébastien smile again. The race had become more mechanical, and we had fallen into the trap of performance at all costs. We were chasing positions in the standings and had forgotten the original plan. When you focus too much on performance, you can sometimes forget who you are and why you do what you do.

As Philippe often said during RAAM, we had to relax! To us, fun was found in the day-to-day, in all our actions and rituals with Sébastien. From day 9 on, we organized surprises, brought out our costumes and created more moments of happiness for Sébastien. This is one of the reasons why Sébastien never gave up — because the whole team was there to cheer him up at all hours of the day and night.

---

[*] YIM, JongEun. Therapeutic Benefits of Laughter in Mental Health: A Theoretical Review. *Tohoku Journal of Experimental Medicine*, 2016, vol. 239, no. 3, pp. 243-249.

LOVE, ALWAYS

So yes, it was fun. But don't think that everything was perfect! Expecting everything to be perfect would not be realistic either. We had a group of 11 people, with different personalities and from different generations; it would be a lie to say that everything was harmonious 100 percent of the time.

For example, Philippe and I had some friction due to a misunderstanding. Admittedly, we were both on adrenaline, and the lack of sleep didn't help either. Nothing abnormal there; in fact, it's quite normal that emotions sometimes get the better of individuals who are very passionate about the mission.

Marcus Aurelius, whom many describe as the greatest emperor to rule Rome, wrote in *Meditations*, "To be free of passion and yet full of love."[*] What a subtle, yet powerful distinction. To me, this passage means putting your ego aside so you can better control your emotions.

Philippe and I talked it out, both admitted our faults and put it behind us. We lowered the emotional temperature and began acting with greater kindness and understanding.

Love also helped Sébastien on the road. I read this somewhere: "Faith is what gets you started. Hope is what keeps you going. Love is what allows you to finish."

From the morning time station to the hotel, Sébastien totaled 102 kilometers to finish the day. As Sébastien recounted in the previous chapter, it took him three hours to complete the last 45 kilometers of the day. I believe that the love the entire team showed him that day kept him going. The kind words, the physical touches, the little treats and the laughter shared along the way made all the difference. All of these small gestures were proof of love, which goes far beyond engagement.

Once at the hotel, and after the Seb to Bed routine was over, I went into the room to talk with Sébastien. I could see the disappointment in his eyes, and after a few moments he burst into tears. He was sorry for letting us down, he was sorry for wanting to quit and he was especially

---

[*] *Marcus Aurelius: Meditations, Book 9*. Oxford University Press, 2013.

sorry for not being able to finish the race. In his mind, at that moment, the race was lost: "I'm going to run out of time."

I hugged him, as my friend needed comfort first. Then I reassured him that it was still possible to finish the race, that we had a plan, and that I would explain it to him when he woke up. I added that the most important thing now was to get five to six hours of sleep to recover. I told him that no matter what happened between now and the finish line, we were proud of him.

As my father, Daniel, taught me so well, living with more love is loving what you do in life. It's about loving your people. And that's ultimately about loving your body of work, loving the person you've become.

I left the room with the door ajar, like a parent watching over a sick child. A few minutes later, once Sébastien was asleep, I noticed that his blood sugar was too high and wanted to make sure that he had injected his insulin. Manon, our diabetes expert, was not there, as she was still caught up in the RV. I went back into the room to check on his insulin pump. Normally, Sébastien, who is a light sleeper, would have woken up at the slightest noise from the door. Not this time!

This episode is one of the most comical of the whole adventure. Up until now, I've never shared this story with Sébastien or even with my partner, Valérie.

As I entered the room, Sébastien was breathing heavily and had both arms over the covers, which reached up to his armpits. This was an unusual sleep position for him, but he'd dozed off as soon as his head hit the pillow. I had no idea where his insulin pump was, but I knew it was somewhere under the sheets. Carefully, I lifted both his arms and then the covers. His arms were limp, and he didn't budge. He was so exhausted that I could have moved him like a marionette.

Once the covers were lifted, I found his pump and saw that, despite his exhaustion, he had taken his insulin. I replaced his blankets and quietly left the room. His diabetes stabilized and he slept like a baby. Thank God, because an enormous challenge awaited him on day 10.

CHAPTER 16

FINAL SPRINT

Sébastien Sasseville

I slept like a log during the Seb to Super Bed. It was restful, uninterrupted and deep. But, let's face it, I was far from bright-eyed and bushy-tailed when I awoke. Gabriel explained the new plan to me and showed me his calculations. I was so happy when I realized that there was a possibility to finish before the time limit. This psychologically revitalized me as I started to believe again that we could make it. And, frankly, I was so grateful that the team hadn't allowed me to give up. I had a golden team.

There is a massive difference between receiving autonomy and taking responsibility. Going beyond your role and serving the mission first. The team's dedication inspired me to dig even deeper, to respond to their relentless engagement with one last burst of energy.

It was 9 p.m. on June 23. We were in Batesville, Indiana, 998 kilometers from the finish line. Outside, everything was in place. The team that would be on duty for the next 12 hours was in V1, and my bike was ready, with Martin holding it 10 meters in front of the car.

One word was on everyone's lips: *execution*.

All efforts would now be directed to finish before the time limit, regardless of ranking, and become a RAAM *finisher*. After all, finishing RAAM is an accomplishment in itself; even for the veterans, the ranking doesn't matter — the real claim to fame is to finish. Finishing this race in 15, 14 or even 13 days would be relatively easy for a good ultra-cyclist. It's the 12-day limit that changes everything and puts you in a class of your own. It's a time limit that requires cyclists to ride a minimum of 400 kilometers per day, with no rest days. Completing the race in 13 or 14 days would allow for a daily distance of 350 kilometers and much more sleep — nothing too demanding for the majority of participants who manage to qualify to enter RAAM.

Rather than put me back on the bike immediately, the team had planned a few extra minutes for a surprise: the party Philippe had requested. In the adjacent room, they had created a festive ambiance with tinsel, music, juice shots and all sorts of things I liked. There were even stuffed cats, as they knew I missed my pets. We made a toast to RAAM, danced for a few seconds and had a good laugh. What a boost to the spirit!

The minutes were all accounted for, so this moment was intense but brief. Psychologically, I was back. I felt driven and inspired. Physically, I felt like I was in decent condition, although, in reality, I was still wrecked. Once the party was over, it was time to get back to the fight. It was 9:30 p.m. I hopped on the bike for another night, another 22-hour stretch. As we walked to the hotel lobby, Gabriel gave me a rundown of the situation. Three days, three clear goals and no room for error.

Objective 1: Batesville, Indiana, to Parkersburg, West Virginia, 400 kilometers

Objective 2: Parkersburg, West Virginia, to Cumberland, Maryland, 300 kilometers

Objective 3: Cumberland, Maryland, to Annapolis, Maryland, 300 kilometers

THE NEXT LOGICAL STEP

Psychologically, I needed that big-picture strategy to build the deep conviction that it was possible. Then my mind went back to the most granular level possible, to a very micro view of the situation.

Execution is the flawless completion of small steps, in the right order, and without any detours. Each step is integrated into a strategic sequence leading to the overall goal.

There was no need to think about the second and third steps at this point. Only completing the first step would grant us access to the next. There was absolutely nothing else in my mind; all my remaining brainpower was dedicated to the next logical step. Execution is about removing distractions. As each stage was relatively tough, the team would draw me a picture of the terrain ahead and I would further break it down into smaller stages. A climb, a flat section, the night block, etc.

Our execution had to be perfect. The distances seemed relatively easy to cover, a sign that my confidence was back. However, RAAM is challenging right up to the end. The last 1,000 kilometers are through the Appalachian Mountains, with endless climbs that are real leg-breakers. And to conclude, one of the most difficult sections of RAAM — a nod by the founders, who wanted the course to be particularly tough at the end, and a deliberate gesture to further restrict accessibility to the sub 12-day club. The founders also wanted the course to include the most beautiful valleys in Maryland, not the fastest route. How nice of them.

Back in the saddle, I knew that the first few hours would be critical and very revealing. How well could the body repair itself in just five hours? We were about to find out whether the resurrection strategy had worked. We were all in. We had put all our chips on those five hours; there was no buffer — I had to ride, and ride well. Thankfully, it seemed to have paid off.

I took the first hour to wake up, ride slowly, reactivate the legs and talk with the team. It was far from a great performance, but I was making progress.

UNINTENTIONAL COMPLACENCY

After a few hours, my speed was still holding steady. Morale was high, and even though we were depending on my legs, the team was determined to do whatever it took to succeed. Execution is also about not letting our commitment to excellence fade during long quests, and giving our best effort until the end. This is about winning the long game, and high-performance teams know how to avoid the unintentional complacency.

Unintentional complacency is very sneaky, and we are all at its mercy, even the most successful among us. Unintentional complacency is most likely when things are going well. When things aren't going well, we're on high alert. When business comes easy, we start cutting corners. Indeed, no one wakes up and says, "Today I'm going to be complacent." But the reality is that we all hate change and are programmed to avoid discomfort. There's nothing wrong with that — it's built into our DNA and is strongly linked to our survival instinct.

Today, frequent social and technological changes force us to act differently. We must bypass our reflex to protect what we believe is true, what we think works, and replace it with a proactive approach to change. Leaders change first, before everyone else, to set the pace. Build the future rather than protect the past. All with balance, of course.

My journey has also taught me that the closer we are to the goal, the harder it is. This is not good or bad, it just is. Resisting unintentional complacency requires conscious, daily effort. We must not only ask the question "What should I do?" but also "How am I going to do it?" We must intentionally commit to excellence every morning.

The "how" does not refer to the technique, but rather to the intention shaping our actions. Do I just want to do my job, or commit to remarkable work today? Are my actions in line with the mission? Am I willing to do difficult and counterintuitive things to grow? What extra step can I take to deliver outstanding work?

Again, what an amazing team I was lucky to have. In the last few days, if there was one thing that touched me, it was the exceptional level of engagement from everyone, right up to the last second. And not just commitment, but something even better — their very best effort. From the first day to the last, I never felt any slack in the team.

MICRO CHANGES ALIGNED WITH THE GOAL

We made another adjustment to our strategy to maximize our chances of success. Orphé, our King's Fool, was brought in as a backup in V1 for the night shifts.

My friendship with Orphé is the longest-standing on the team. He's a close friend, someone with whom I've had a ton of fun — there are many stories I can't tell here! He's a joker, but he is also much, much more. Well read, he quotes characters like Napoleon in his everyday conversations. He brought disguises with him to make me laugh during the race. He's a great cook, but he's also an engineer by training, and he's a very good mechanic. He always made the team laugh, and his presence was appreciated by all. Orphé was a favorite of the whole team, but also the pest we had to deal with. What a character!

Orphé's antics to make Sébastien laugh during the final stretch.

The hours between midnight and 5 a.m. were always extremely difficult. I was fighting sleep and struggling to stay awake. Orphé had spent most of his time driving the RV and taking care of the vehicles. His new mission was to entertain me at night to keep me awake. In a team, everyone is important and esveryone as a role to play. Some team members often work in the shadows, but they are just as important. And sometimes, like in the present case, team members must come out of the shadows and shine.

In execution mode, frequent micro-adjustments are essential. Conversely, it's too late for big changes in the strategy, unless there's a safety issue. At the end of the road, you must work with what you have and live with some imperfections. Wanting to change everything at this point would only slow the team down unnecessarily, or even put the mission at risk. Execution is not a time to perfect the plan, it is a time to get to the goal, period. Keep a steady pace; stay positive and keep moving forward with consistency.

CREATE FAVORABLE CIRCUMSTANCES

The mini-party after my five-hour "night"; the status report delivered by Gabriel; the division of task into smaller blocks; the shift of the team into a more festive mode; the return to the original sleep strategy — we did everything possible to create a climate conducive to our success.

This is an important principle in sports and is equally true for our personal and professional lives: to focus on creating favorable circumstances. Self-awareness is the first step. In what type of environment do I perform better? What are the perfect conditions for my success? Next, to succeed, one must make a conscious effort to create these circumstances. There's nothing complicated here, but you must take the time to stop, think and do what's necessary. The important thing in life is not knowing what to do, it's doing what you must!

To illustrate this, I use my own example — my job as a motivational and business speaker. The hour I spend onstage is a tiny fraction of my work week, but it's the part I'm judged on. My job is to be remarkable for an hour.

Of course, the preparatory calls with clients, the follow-ups, the professionalism at all stages of the collaboration, the preparation and research for the customization of each keynote are all important. But in the end, the audience doesn't see any of it. For the audience, the entire contact with me is restricted to my presence onstage, and that is what they will judge.

To create favorable circumstances, I try to speak in the morning. If given the choice, my absolute favorite time slot to speak is between 10 a.m. and noon. That is when I am most productive intellectually. The sound check is done the day before so there aren't any worries on the day of the event.

The morning of a keynote, I work out for 30 minutes at most. The point is not to improve my future performance, but rather to oxygenize my brain to maximize my intellectual output for the day. As an aside, when you exercise to feel good today, rather than to achieve a result in six months, it's much easier to motivate yourself.

Next, I eat breakfast in my hotel room and review my notes. An hour or two before my keynote, I go down to the meeting room to attend part of the meeting to get the pulse of the group.

All this logic also applies to a high-performing team. What are the right environment and parameters the team needs to succeed? Have we already put these conditions in writing?

KNOW YOUR FIRST DOMINO

To execute well, you must also identify your first domino. Imagine dominoes carefully lined up, one centimeter apart. You have spent many minutes meticulously placing them, one by one, either in a long straight line or in a complex pattern with curves. Then comes the fateful moment: You push the first domino and trigger a chain reaction.

The first domino kicks off the whole process. Everyone's first domino may differ. Maybe yours is to exercise, or to plan your week on Sunday night, or to take a moment by the lake to meditate.

My first domino is sleep. Sleep is my religion. Without perfect sleep, that perfect morning topped with a killer performance onstage doesn't exist. So, the night before, I go to bed early. Executing is mostly about learning to say no. No socializing or visiting the city I'm in. Saying no is respecting your needs, your success, your clients and the people you ought to serve. Saying no is respect. It's a powerful gesture.

As I live with type 1 diabetes, good control of my blood sugar is peremptory to a good night's sleep. To go to bed with stable blood sugar levels, it is best to eat early, so that I have time to stabilize my blood sugar levels before bedtime if necessary. Choosing a healthy meal also makes it easier to manage my blood sugar. It goes without saying that I don't drink alcohol the night before, because even in small doses, alcohol has an impact on sleep.

So if you hire me to speak at your next annual meeting, and the night before you see me eating a salad and pasta with a glass of water at 5 p.m., I'm already at work. I am creating a climate that is conducive to my performance. I have identified my first domino, and I am maximizing my chances of success for my performance the next day.

PART IV

CELEBRATING THE JOURNEY

> I cannot live without champagne.
> If I win, I deserve it; if I lose, I need it.
>
> — NAPOLEON BONAPARTE, FORMER FRENCH
> MILITARY GENERAL AND STATESMAN

CHAPTER 17

SMALL THINGS ARE BIG THINGS

Gabriel Renaud

We were less than 1,000 kilometers from the goal. So close and yet so far. Normally, three days to cover 1,000 kilometers would be a piece of cake for Sébastien, but this was different. Other competitors were pulling out of the race one after another. The 2022 race had been marked by overwhelming heat. The Appalachians were waiting for us, with hard climbs, some of them at a 10 percent incline, and Sébastien's physical condition was shaky.

At this point, the important thing was for Sébastien to get back on his bike and regain his confidence. After a collapse, doubt is an athlete's worst enemy. The remedy was to gradually regain his belief in himself on the bike. Fortunately, the first night after the reset strategy went well and Sébastien rode over 250 kilometers. He was far from being in fine shape, but he was moving steadily at a more than respectable pace for a guy who was completely wiped out the night before.

More than ever, the role of the team was crucial to the success of the mission. On day 10, with each passing hour, Sébastien was again flirting with his breaking point. The more the day progressed, the more Sébastien started to sway on the bike. Each pedal stroke became more and more painful. Again, the rubber band was almost stretched to its limit.

It's fascinating to see how humans come to the aid of others when they're in need. Starting on day 10, the team sometimes skipped their own rest to come and cheer Sébastien on the course. The crew from the night shift would stay up during the day to get him ice cream or fried chicken. Sébastien doesn't eat a lot of meat, but during RAAM, he gulped down everything he was given! The day crew would also come out on the road at night to cheer him on. The simple things, heartfelt and genuine gestures, really made a difference for Sébastien. He successfully completed his first goal, covering 400 kilometers that day. Sébastien was back in 12th place.

Philippe hands fried chicken to Sébastien. Sébastien always loved it when we surprised him with treats.

Our athlete was still physically broken, but psychologically, these small actions coming from our hearts did him good. Actions that also included a few disguises, obviously provided by Orphé, to make him laugh in passing. Sébastien felt supported by the whole team at all times of the day. His mind could no longer wander into hallucinations, because we were always on the move with him, pulling him back to reality. Trust me, he sure was aware he was racing RAAM at this point!

We also looked for other marginal, but important, gains. We adapted some of our processes during our last two Seb to Beds to be even more efficient. For example, I spoon-fed Sébastien on the massage table while Marie-Michèle treated him. Also, Sébastien started using his spare bike on the steep climbs and descents of the Appalachian Mountains. It was a lighter, more responsive bike, so we saved more precious minutes. Up against the wall like we were, these small details were instrumental to our chances for success. With no time to spare, and no certainty we would finish in time, every second counted.

How you execute the details of a plan is indicative of how you perform with respect to the big picture. It's the little details that enable big success. Doing the fundamentals right is always the best strategy. It's also the small details that touch our hearts. All of this made a difference for Sébastien, as he felt loved and supported by his family. We indeed had gone from strangers, to a team, to family.

WE ARE ALL LEADERS

On day 11, another team put out a call for help in the RAAM team chat group. The team was desperately looking for a medical professional to treat their athlete, who had severe back pain. Interestingly, this athlete was in 11th place, right in front of Sébastien, about 48 kilometers ahead of us. Without hesitation, the V1 team volunteered to help. Marie-Michèle, who was in V1, already had all her physiotherapy equipment with her. The V1 team saw a need and took action. It was a great demonstration of leadership.

Leadership is not reserved for the elite or those at the top of the organizational chart. Leadership is a behavior, not a title. The people present simply chose to help because the circumstances demanded it. Situations like these require leadership. When a difficult situation arises in your business or in your family, someone must have the courage to stand up and address the problem. That is a leadership moment. Sometimes we wait, thinking that it should be the person in authority who has to do it; but every individual can exercise leadership, regardless of their title.[*]

The struggling athlete was in very poor shape. Without Marie-Michèle's help, he confessed that he probably wouldn't have been able to finish the race. This moment is a great source of pride for the entire team, because rather than seeing an opportunity to move up in the rankings, we saw an opportunity to help another person. Marie-Michèle's gesture and

---

[*] KIMSEY-HOUSE, Karen, and KIMSEY-HOUSE, Henry. *Co-Active Leadership: Five Ways to Lead*. Berrett-Koehler, 2021.

leadership reflected on our entire team. Our sportsmanship was highlighted on RAAM's social networks, and we received many accolades for our attitude. For me, these were the fruits of all the time invested in defining our culture, who we wanted to be, what we wanted to be remembered for and how we wanted to behave amongst ourselves and with others.

ACTION INSPIRES ACTION

On day 1, a member of another team asked if he could borrow a tool. We were on our way to join Sébastien after a shift change. Needless to say, we were in a hurry. However, Philippe turned to me and said: "We'll be happy if a team helps us out later — that's karma."

Sometimes when you help, there is a direct benefit to you; sometimes not. In the end, we didn't need help from another team. However, we did receive a few warnings from the officials without ever receiving a penalty. RAAM comes with a 60-page rule book. Most rules are for everyone's safety. For example, if there is no sufficient shoulder to stop and not obstruct the road, a support vehicle isn't allowed to stop. We obeyed the rules as best as we could, but as all teams, we made a few mistakes. Were the officials more lenient on us because we exemplified good sportsmanship?

Karma or not, helping was in our nature. It was part of the collaborative pillar of our culture. When a leader embodies generosity like Philippe did, it inspires others to do the same. The one you help will be more likely to give to the next in need. Such actions spread throughout the organization and inspire even more people to emulate these behaviors.

Audrey Hepburn said, "You have two hands, one for yourself and one for helping others." Every day, we all have the opportunity to perform an act of generosity. In addition, helping others is one of the best ways to cultivate happiness in our daily lives.[*] It is also a great way to enrich our relationships and build new ones.

---

[*] PARK, Soyoung Q., KAHNT, Thorsten, DOGAN, Azade, et al. A Neural Link Between Generosity and Happiness. *Nature Communications*, 2017, vol. 8, no. 1, pp. 1-10.

FINDING JOY

In the last days of the race, a lightness settled into the team. Yes, the mission was paramount, but it couldn't be all-consuming; little things, like renaming V1 the "love van," added to our happiness. The love van became a central point of conversation and a never-ending source of jokes. After all, V1 was always behind Sébastien, on the move 24/7 and always fully staffed. It was the most central part of our logistics.

It all started when we renamed the small resting area "the master bedroom." Little by little, Philippe, Marie-Michèle and Valérie took great pleasure in "renovating" and furnishing the love van. With each new shift, Philippe would say he had done improvements in his van. Eventually, we also put in a shower, a pantry, a closet, a fridge, a sofa bed and even a clothesline.

There were several other examples of small daily joys within the team. Dan practiced street photography, taking photos of people he met. Philippe would call his girlfriend every day. He would tell us, "I'm off for 20 minutes." Martin, on the other hand, would recharge at the hotel pool or go for a run.

During RAAM, our energies were mainly directed towards one thing: fulfilling the mission. When we are so deeply committed to a mission, our tendency is to put all our energies into it, sometimes forgetting that life is made of many interrelated parts. The classic example is the professional who invests all their energy in their work while forgetting to maintain their health, relationships and the other pillars of their life.

All aspects of our lives have an impact on each other. When one's health or relationships begin to suffer, so will one's work, even if we put all our energy into it. It was our balanced approach that enabled us to maintain a healthy equilibrium and reduce the level of tension inherent to RAAM.

TIME TO SHINE

The plan was going well so far. The next day, Sébastien once again managed to reach the daily goal, this time of 300 kilometers. We were about 30 minutes ahead of the target I had set. However, nothing was won yet.

The ultimate test was waiting for us on the last night. It was four massive climbs in Maryland, before a detour through Pennsylvania and a second and final entry into Maryland.

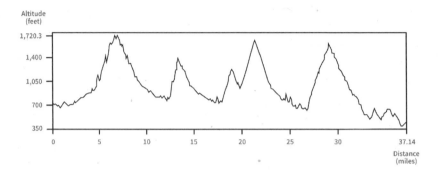

The four climbs in Maryland. Five kilometers of uphill climbs, at a 10 percent grade, culminating at an altitude of about 550 meters. Philippe and I knew that this was what it would all come down to. If Sébastien could get through those bumps, we would finish RAAM.

We did a last team huddle at the last Seb to Bed. I presented the team with my calculations for the last day, and we decided to wake Sébastien up 30 minutes earlier than planned to give ourselves some extra margin. As I woke Sébastien up, I simply told him, "Time to shine. If you make it through the night, you'll be a RAAM finisher!"

When Sébastien left the hotel, I was truly nervous. I was hoping that the adrenaline from the last day would give him the boost he needed to succeed, but at the same time I had my doubts. The last few climbs were real leg-breakers. That night, V2 decided to go and cheer Sébastien on at the side of the road. I was part of that team. The team was ready to give everything they had for the final hours of the race.

Once again, the small gestures made all the difference. To divert his attention from the pain, I ran alongside Sébastien during these tough ascents, which were the most difficult of the Appalachians. I didn't leave him for one second. Meanwhile, other team members were waiting for him at the top of a climb. They had even gathered the partygoers from the hostel located at the top of the hill to cheer him on!

SMALL THINGS ARE BIG THINGS

To keep Sébastien entertained, Gabriel ran alongside him through some of the toughest Appalachian climbs.

Once at the top of the third of four climbs, I looked at the clock. It was midnight. Sébastien seemed to have found a new energy. Barring a catastrophe, he was going to be a RAAM finisher.

CHAPTER 18

THE FINISH LINE

Sébastien Sasseville

It was a beautiful sight in the early morning of day 12. A small section of the course passed through Pennsylvania, and we briefly exited Maryland at sunrise. The scenery was more beautiful than a postcard. Perfectly manicured farms, white wooden fences, cows grazing, mist, dew and the sun breaking through the dawn gently with orange rays. I had to cross the finish line before 4 p.m. that day.

We were still at least 250 kilometers from the finish line. In my earpiece I heard, "Congratulations, Sébastien." I didn't understand what Philippe meant. He added: "Tonight you saved our RAAM." I remember that moment almost as clearly as the finish line, because, in a way, it was a finish line. Philippe had been apprehensive about the final climbs; the rubber band could have snapped again. All that was now behind us.

Although many moments of RAAM, and even whole days, are a blur, I have very clear memories of specific or decisive events. This moment was very emotional for me, and it spread to everyone in V1. We were starting to feel a great sense of pride. Even though we had to stay on our toes until the end, we felt that we would finish the race.

We were all aware that our great adventure would soon be over. I had been working on the project for over a year. We'd had 23 weekly meetings, and in just 72 hours we would be back home with unforgettable memories.

THE FINISH LINE

In the months following the return, several team members explained to me that they sometimes found it difficult to recount their experience. You had to be there, as they say. There are things that cannot be explained; you live them, you grow from the experience, and those memories are ours to cherish.

Still, it was time for it to end. A few days earlier, I had burst into tears when I saw a dead cat on the road, hit by a car. I was so sad that someone had lost their cat.

At least this emotional roller coaster was fun for the crew — there were certainly some laughs at my expense in V1!

As I described earlier, the last few miles are far from easy. That's by design. Early in the morning of June 26, we were under the impression that we had plenty of time to complete the race. I was told many times to "have fun" and "enjoy it, it will be over soon." The reality is that as I approached the first few hills, and the next few, and the other hills after that, my energy level dropped off. I rode silently, concentrating on each pedal stroke, not smiling much . . .

Everything indicated that we would arrive before the time limit, but the question remained: Had we received any penalties? As Gabriel mentioned in the last chapter, we hadn't yet, but we only got confirmation of this at the end of the race. Consequently, there was still some doubt. We decided not to slow down, and to give it our all until the end. Yes, I had to enjoy the moment, but this was certainly not the time to slow down the pace. With 50 kilometers to go, now much closer to the coast, the terrain finally smoothed out.

RAAM has two finish lines. The first is located at Rams Head Roadhouse, about 15 kilometers from the second and final finish line, in Annapolis. While it is cause for much celebration, the first finish line is only a line and two orange cones in the middle of nowhere.

This first line at Rams Head Roadhouse is the official finish, and the race technically ends here. So why bother with a second finish line? It's purely a safety measure, as traffic is heavier as you get closer to the city. In the event that some participants may arrive close to each other, the final sprint takes place before Rams Head Roadhouse on a quiet country road. After the first finish line, you are no longer allowed to overtake your competitors. To officially become a RAAM finisher, however, participants must make their way from the first finish line to the second finish line. A few kilometers from the second finish line, in Annapolis, we had to make a mandatory stop at a gas station. Here, an official RAAM vehicle was waiting for us. The last kilometers are done under escort, for a triumphant arrival on City Dock, on the edge of the Atlantic Ocean. There, a crowd and the RAAM organization awaited us for a proper celebration.

My arrival at Rams Head Roadhouse, the official finish line. From that point on, it was in the bag!

Our team was all there to celebrate at the first finish line.

RAAM is not the Super Bowl. The finish line is a very special moment for the participants, but the crowds are not large. When 5,000 people participate in a major marathon, that's 5,000 families, friends and spouses lining the finish line. With 33 participants in the 2022 solo event, 19 of whom dropped out along the way, that leaves us with 14 cyclists crossing

THE FINISH LINE

a finish line in a 48-hour period. Some arrive in Annapolis in the middle of the night, so other than their support crew and RAAM staff, there's no one to greet them with a roar.

I finished on a sunny Sunday afternoon. There were a lot of passersby and tourists, so we were fortunate to have a nice welcome. Once we crossed that second finish line and confirmed that we had not received any penalties, it was official. After so much work, the dream had come true.

We completed RAAM in 11 days, 22 hours and 25 minutes, in 5th place out of 14 in the men's under-50 category, and 12th place overall.

Had we been 95 minutes slower, and it would have been a DNF. All those minutes gained here and there and every detail we paid attention to is what made us successful.

Once off the bike, each rider is invited to a large stage for the official photo, presentation of a medal and a personalized commemorative plaque certifying a completed RAAM.

Onstage, each participant is interviewed by George Thomas, a legend in the world of ultra-cycling. He asked me about the major problems we had to overcome. As I tried to articulate my answer, I began to hear laughter from the team. I told George that I thought everything had gone well, and that there had been no major glitches. Instantly, the team shouted in unison, "He doesn't know!" I had indeed just learned of the RV's adventures a few minutes earlier. This amused George, and he mentioned that if the problems didn't make it to the athlete, it was a sign that the team had done a tremendous job. He was right.

When I went onstage, the crowd applauded. Once the medal was around my neck, a team photo followed. George invited the whole team to come onstage, but at this point the crowd was silent, as if it was just a formality.

This didn't resonate with me at all. I started clapping and shouting at the top of my lungs. Team recognition had been an integral part of our entire preparation; it wasn't going to stop after the finish line. The crowd was surprised at first by my burst of enthusiasm, but then started to applaud with excitement.

RECOGNITION AS A HABIT

George noticed how important team appreciation was to me, so he asked me a few questions about it. In fact, most of my interview was about the team.* I was not in a state to eloquently articulate my thoughts, but I knew that our success was shared and collective. I knew that without them I could never have made it. To me, we were all equal teammates who had just accomplished something great together. I didn't feel like my role was any more or less important than that of the trailer driver or the cook.

The team was not surprised by my responses and the recognition I was offering. For almost a year, gratitude was part of our DNA. Every week, in small gestures, thoughts, words and thanks, Gabriel and I expressed to the team how grateful we were for the work they were doing.

The habit had become contagious. We often think of recognition as a gesture from the employer to the employee. Recognition between colleagues is also very important in developing a culture of excellence.

The whole team was here by choice. When one of us spent many hours on a task, the others would not fail to recognize it. Each of us had at heart a common objective, albeit for different reasons, but the desire to succeed was shared by all. When a team member's work brought us a little closer to the goal, it was always noticed and deeply appreciated, and everyone insisted on sharing their gratitude.

A moment of celebration on stage with the team.

---

* Watch the full interview here: "RAAM 2022 Finish Line: 661 — Sebastien Sasseville — Quebec," https://www.youtube.com/watch?v=4giDP-b5stQ.

It's well documented that recognition is one of the main pillars of engagement.* Most companies have extensive recognition programs, from e-cards to trips to Hawaii, and these programs certainly play a role in building engagement. But recognition doesn't have to cost a lot of money. In fact, the greatest impact can be had for free. A heartfelt thank you, or spending time with someone can go a long way. Provided, that is, that it's sincere and not done from a sense of obligation.

CUSTOMIZE RECOGNITION

I've always noticed that natural leaders have a keen interest in others. The more senior managers I meet, the more questions they ask about me. Empathy is often identified as the most important quality in a leader.** This opens the door to personalizing recognition.

Personalizing recognition means offering recognition tailored to the recipient and their unique contribution. This requires more work, more listening and a real interest in people.

To choose the right form of recognition, you must know the recipients, their motivations. You must be interested in their lives, their interests, their personal mission, their convictions, their ambitions. It is also necessary to personalize the approach and the coaching for each person. It's a mark of respect for their differences and strengths for which we have chosen them.

Personalizing recognition also means noticing that their effort went beyond expectations, and that the effort was a challenge for that individual.

---

*   BRADLER, Christiane, DUR, Robert, NECKERMANN, Susanne, et al. Employee Recognition and Performance: A Field Experiment. *Management Science*, 2016, vol. 62, no. 11, pp. 3085-3099.

** GENTRY, William A., WEBER, Todd J., and SADRI, Golnaz. Empathy in the Workplace: A Tool for Effective Leadership. *Annual Conference of the Society of Industrial Organizational Psychology*, April 2007, New York, NY.

REWARDING BEHAVIORS

By contrast, in our team we resisted the temptation to offer too much recognition. Being competitive athletes, we don't really believe in participation medals. It was very important for us to recognize outstanding contributions and exceptional efforts because we knew it would have a ripple effect. Recognition is also a tool to promote the behaviors and the attitudes that we want to see in the organization. Recognition must be seen by the manager as a performance tool, not just a feel-good treat.

In fact, it is important to understand this very powerful logic: recognition creates engagement, and engagement creates performance. Rewarding results, numbers, dollars and sales is universal and generally mastered by all companies. Rewarding the behaviors that lead to these results is often forgotten.

There's nothing wrong with rewarding numbers, but numbers are the consequence of behaviors and attitudes. Especially in an age where success and performance are celebrated to an excess, it's important to put the summit of the mountain aside momentarily and reward growth habits and those good behaviors and attitudes that ground success.

It's essential to underline the effort, the progress and the energy expended to get the job done. We must recognize the quality of the work, the attitude, the interpersonal skills and the human values that support and are constitutive of the desired culture. All of this should be recognized, rather than just the result. The employer who recognizes the right behavior ensures not only that the team moves in the right direction, but that, more importantly, it does so in the right manner, to build lasting success.

Recognition offered in the moment and spontaneously is often the most impactful. Hence the importance of having leaders "on the floor" who are present to what is really going on.

Once our finish line celebrations were over, we all headed to the hotel, the last part of the journey. The bees never stopped being extraordinary, and their mission was not quite over.

CHAPTER 19

HONORING THE JOURNEY

Gabriel Renaud

Megaprojects don't end when the spotlights go out. In the hotel parking lot, Martin and Philippe had to sort out equipment, parts and tools, as well as dismantle the bikes to put them in their transport box. We also had to empty and clean the RV. Réjean and I had to return the minivans to the rental agency. The rest of the team was busy sorting out the clothes and equipment that had been scattered around throughout the vehicles over the last 12 days. In short, no rest for the weary!

In the evening, we had our first meal all together since Oceanside. What a joy it was to be able to toast our success! The next day we left Annapolis early. Twelve hours later, we were all back home.

LIVE IN THE MOMENT

Since the celebration was short-lived in Annapolis, we organized a reunion weekend at a cottage three months after returning. It was a chance to reminisce and a time to reconnect. Sports, laughter and good food were the order of the day. It was even an opportunity to go cycling together.

Despite our best efforts to find a date that was ideal for everyone, three members of the team couldn't make it. The last time the whole team was together was at the dinner in Annapolis. Often, we have memorable experiences with a group but, despite our best intentions, are unable to all come together to see each other again. Such is life.

This taught me how important it is to cherish the moments when a group is all together. How important it is to live in the present moment. A team is dynamic and changes constantly; there are departures, arrivals and absences. Without realizing it at the time, there are many moments that are last times. That's why it's essential to appreciate when we're together with those we love.

THE BEST ANECDOTES

Our team weekend at the cottage was also an opportunity to reminisce about our best RAAM stories. We laughed so much that Sébastien and I thought it would be a crime not to share some of them.

We'll limit ourselves to 13 anecdotes — one for the departure day, and one for each day on the road.

Please enjoy!

DEPARTURE DAY: A VOLCANO LIKE NO OTHER

Martin and Réjean were filling up the RV's water tank with the Airbnb's garden hose while talking quietly. The day was beautiful, and Manon was busy inside, organizing the kitchen.

Suddenly, Manon seemed panicked. She shouted, "Guys, come here now! I think there is something wrong!"

A horrible sewage odor had invaded the RV. Outside, gray water was gushing out from the top chimney like a volcano. Martin came running. He flung open the door of the RV and was shocked to find the toilet was also overflowing.

They grabbed all the paper towels they could find and searched for the cause of the problem. They soon realized that they were filling the wastewater tank instead of the clean water tank, pushing all the gray water up and out!

All this happened while the TV crew was interviewing Manon about her role as a cook. Suffice to say, their inspiration was cut short. After disinfecting everything, Martin and Réjean had to go to a campground to empty the gray water tanks that they had filled to the brim.

DAY 1: WHAT YOU DON'T KNOW WON'T HURT YOU

As we were stopping for our first Seb to Bed, we wanted everything to be perfect for Sébastien, who had just ridden 550 kilometers in 22 hours. But as we entered the motel room in Salome in the middle of the desert, Dan immediately spotted some cockroaches by the nightstand. They were dead, but still, it was disgusting.

It didn't matter, as long as the rest of the room was clean. Dan lifted the sheets ... There were five large cockroaches on the bed.

We were very tired, but as you can imagine, nobody felt like sleeping there. Unfortunately, we had no choice. We had to rest; we had just spent almost 30 hours awake. We cleaned the bed and slept on top of the sheets, covering ourselves with sleeping bags. Fortunately, we didn't find any cockroaches in Sébastien's room. In fact, we didn't tell him about what we had seen. He had to rest!

DAY 2: A BEDTIME STORY

The first sleep stop of the RV was in a Walmart parking lot. In the desert, even the nighttime temperature was close to 30 degrees Celsius, and our air conditioner was not working. Moreover, with all the luggage, we did not have enough beds on board for all five members of the team.

Réjean is never short of solutions. Exasperated by the heat, he picked up his sleeping bag to go sleep under the stars ... on the roof of the RV! Luckily there were no mosquitoes, and he didn't fall off the roof. In the end, Réjean slept so well that he repeated the experience three times during the trip.

DAY 3: CIAO BYE!

While RAAM was taking place, other cyclists were competing in the Race Across the West (RAW). This is a similar event, but much shorter (1,500 kilometers). The race has the same starting line, begins on the same day as RAAM and uses the same route. RAW ends in Durango, Colorado, which is the first cut-off point for RAAM.

One RAW participant was Italian. On day 3, Sébastien cycled alongside him for a short while. Seeming to be somewhat disoriented, and a bit full of himself, the Italian asked Sébastien, "Do you want to race?"

Knowing that he had to ride 3,500 kilometers more than this fool, Sébastien declined.

We ran into this smarty-pants a few more times while he was zigzagging from left to right and wasting a lot of energy. Sébastien found him dangerous and kept his distance. On the last few climbs to Durango, Sébastien passed him at high speed to send him a message, and we never saw him again.

DAY 4: THE GREAT BEET DECEPTION

The beet powder story was a running joke during the early days of our RAAM. Beet juice has been found to increase athletic performance. Among other things, beets promote oxygen delivery to the muscles. The team foresaw only marginal gains coming from this, but Sébastien was very keen on his beet juice. He had a container full of it in powder form that we were to mix with water. However, we accidentally spilled it and lost it all when leaving for Oceanside. We felt terrible.

Every time Sébastien asked for beet juice during the first few days of the race, Philippe would reply, "Coming right up!" Philippe didn't know how to tell him that we had lost the powder, and he was counting on Sébastien's exhaustion and hoping that he would just forget.

Well, believe it or not, Philippe's strategy worked five or six times, each time becoming even funnier. Finally, on day four, Philippe told him that we had spilled the beet concentrate in Oceanside, and that we never actually had any in V1. Sébastien simply replied, "Well, I won't have any, then!"

A few days later, while rummaging through the RV supplies, the team found another jar. We prepared a bottle for Sébastien without warning him of the contents. You should have seen the bafflement in his face. He thought he was losing his mind.

DAY 5: WOULD YOU RATHER

During the night, we frequently played games with Sébastien to keep him awake. It was our way of accompanying him through the darkness. Our favorite game was "would you rather," which consists of choosing which of two options you prefer. Needless to say, the more horrible the choices are, the more fun the game is. For example: "Would you rather wear oven mitts 24 hours a day for the rest of your life or wear ski boots 24 hours a day for the rest of your life?" Usually, we were the ones giving the choices, because Sébastien was too tired to think and craft good choices.

However, this night he decided that he was the one giving the choices. His first question was, "Would you rather spend the rest of your life with spaghetti feet or without a serious illness?" Exhausted, Sébastien didn't really offer a difficult choice! Marie-Michèle laughed hard while trying to explain to him why his choices didn't make sense. That was a short round.

DAY 6: BEWARE OF DOG

It was quite late at night and Sébastien was riding very slowly. Réjean was driving V1 in direct follow when he suddenly saw an animal coming out of the ditch.

In a fraction of a second, Réjean realized that it was a large pit bull type of dog. The rabid beast ran fiercely towards Sébastien, barking aggressively. Sébastien's reaction was instantaneous: he accelerated to nearly 40 km/h. The V1 members had never seen Sébastien ride so fast except on the downhill. According to Réjean, "Sébastien's screams, combined with the dog's barking, created quite a cacophony in the car's headset. It was something else!"

The animal even tried to grab one of Sébastien's legs but didn't succeed. After a few hundred meters, it gave up. What a relief! However, now that we knew he had it in him, Sébastien was teased and asked to go faster several times that night.

DAY 7: HAVE YOUR CAKE AND EAT IT TOO

In an on-camera interview with Marc-Antoine on day 7, Sébastien said, "My favorite part of RAAM so far has been eating carrot cake" — his favorite dessert. This statement did not fall on deaf ears: Manon knew he hadn't had any yet. Manon didn't think for a minute this was delusion from fatigue; she saw it as a message. Sébastien was still able to be funny! Message received.

Manon immediately got to work. She baked the precious dessert despite the heat and humidity and the limited space of the RV. I came to see her — it must have been 38 degrees with the heat of the oven and the sun. She was very hot and later admitted to me that there was probably a drop of sweat or two in that cake. The next day, Sébastien finally had his cake. I can assure you that Manon's carrot cake was appreciated by all. But the team tried to leave most of it for Sébastien...except Marie-Michèle!

DAY 8: WHEN THE CAT IS AWAY, THE MICE WILL PLAY

The V1 team needed to stock up on supplies to get through the day. Since Sébastien just had to keep going straight for 15 kilometers, it was the perfect time to go to the grocery store. Philippe said to Sébastien, "Keep riding and we'll come back and find you."

Back on the route after their detour, V1 advanced until the team realized that something wasn't right. According to their phone's locator, Sébastien was right behind them. But they hadn't yet passed him on the road. Philippe raised his head, saw Sébastien through the window of V1 and shouted to Valérie: "Stop the van!" No sooner said than done. Philippe hopped out of the car and ran towards Sébastien.

Guess what Sébastien was doing? He was hiding! He said he was looking at "the statistics on his watch." He had found a small logging road; he was deep in the trees. He was exhausted and had taken advantage of the time away from the team to take an extra break. We really couldn't leave him alone anymore!

DAY 9: THE GOOD, THE BAD AND THE UGLY

Philippe gave a Styrofoam cup filled with food to Sébastien. Normally, Sébastien always handed his empty cup back to the team through the window of the vehicle while riding. But this time, V1 had to stop for a moment, so Philippe told him to just drop it on the shoulder and we would pick it up so he wouldn't lose time.

Sébastien was again alone on the road. After eating everything, looking for any excuse to stop, he came to a halt to put the cup on the ground. He then put a rock in it so it wouldn't blow away.

A few moments later, V1 retrieved it and quickly deduced what Sébastien had done. A little amused, but definitely not happy that Sébastien had stopped, they caught up to him: "Did you really stop to put a rock in the cup?"

Sébastien replied, "It would have blown away in the wind, I don't want to look like a hillbilly!" He gave us a good laugh, but we realized that we really needed to watch him closely so he wouldn't stop for no reason.

DAY 10: GONE LIKE THE WIND

Throughout RAAM, we stopped at hotels and motels of all kinds. First, there were the Arizona cockroaches. In Colorado we had a live chicken market in the motel parking lot. We were a long way from the Ritz!

Then, in Kansas, we stopped at a completely empty motel in the middle of a ghost town. A few windows were boarded up, and the place looked sort of scary. There was only one vehicle in the parking lot, the owner's white minivan. The establishment didn't feel overly safe; however, the rooms were very clean.

On day 10, at a somewhat run-down motel in Ohio, we observed strange individuals and behavior to say the least . . . the motel was a gathering place for what appeared to be drug dealers. A police car would come around the parking lot frequently. Later in the evening, a motel employee took all the furniture out of a room and burned it outside. Let's just say we've never checked out so quickly!

DAY 11: BLACK AND WHITE

The finish line was near, and Sébastien was hanging on by a thread — physically and emotionally. For example, the day before, he had burst into tears on his bike after seeing a cat that had been hit by a car.

Another cat had unfortunately met the same fate on day 11. As he passed by, Sébastien began to come apart emotionally again. Réjean was driving V1 and said to him: "Don't worry Sébastien, it's a skunk." Sébastien replied, "Are you sure?" "Yes, 100 percent sure, it was a skunk." The poor thing was indeed black and white. "Are you really, really sure? It really looked like a cat." "I'm telling you, Sébastien, it was a skunk. "Well, in that case, it's okay!"

Sébastien continued his way calmly, quickly forgetting what he had seen. On the way back home, Réjean admitted that it was indeed a cat.

ARRIVAL DAY: PARTY ANIMAL

After the team dinner in Annapolis, we went out for ice cream. We were all exhausted, so we went home very early after that. Dan, Orphé and Marc-Antoine shared a room. After a few beers, Dan was outraged that we weren't celebrating more. He was pacing the room and trying to convince his roommates to get out of bed. "You guys can't do this to me! Why aren't we at the bar? This is unacceptable! I can't believe it!"

Marc-Antoine and Orphé were trying to sleep, but their laughter at poor Dan kept them awake. The next day, they were quick to tell the whole team about it at breakfast. They couldn't keep this good story to themselves!

CHAPTER 20

WHAT'S LEFT OF IT?

Gabriel Renaud

The weekend at the cottage, this final time together recounting stories and anecdotes, marked the end of the adventure.

It goes without saying that while life goes on, we all grew tremendously from this experience. So today, what remains of this journey? What has been its lasting impact? The best people to answer this question are the members of the team.

Without the 10 other members of the team, none of this would have been possible. Each was open to whatever was asked of them, and they welcomed all of our initiatives. With them, we created unforgettable memories. Because of them, Sébastien and I had material to write a book that, we certainly hope, will have an impact on those who read it. I have them all in my heart, and before they offer a few words of their own, I want to express my sincerest thanks once again.

We asked each of them to write a few words on their experience, what they have learned, specific moments they will cherish and the key lessons learned. Now, over to them.

DAN APONTE, PHOTOGRAPHER, DRIVER AND NAVIGATOR

"It's hard to pinpoint one particular event as my defining experience during the race — there are so many. This journey, as well as last year's ride across Canada, has revealed strengths that I possess, but rarely exploit. While I am often hesitant to show leadership and make decisions, on several occasions this year and last, I was able to contribute to critical decisions that helped the team navigate critical situations. The experience reminded me that, when I put the needs of others before my own, and when I work with a team towards a goal bigger than myself, I am the happiest and give my best. Experiences like RAAM are learning opportunities that reveal a person's true nature and character. These lessons have already had profound effects on my short- and long-term goals, as well as how I handle my own experiences."

MANON GAUTHIER, COOK AND DIABETES SPECIALIST, ADMINISTRATION

"The RAAM team adventure was an extraordinary experience that I was not able to fully grasp in the days following the race. It was so intense and rich that it took some time to decant and to be able to see the whole picture. Now I can say that it expanded my comfort zone even more. I was confident that I would be able to adapt to all the needs and unforeseen events that would come our way. The experience confirmed this and gave me confidence that I would be able to accomplish other adventures or effectively deal with whatever crazy events life throws my way. This experience has also allowed me to develop a few abilities that are still what I call my zone of effort, and that would benefit from further development. It's a work in progress. Finally, I realized that when I was in the eye of the storm, in the action and 'focused' on accomplishing my role in the mission, I did not realize the magnitude of what we accomplished. I realized it much later, and I am very proud of it. To sum up, I am left with greater confidence, personal growth and pride."

MARC-ANTOINE LEGAULT-FRENETTE, VIDEOGRAPHER

"Having been a videographer for 16 years, RAAM has allowed me to push my art to another level, a level I wasn't even aware I could go to. RAAM has been a unique life experience for many reasons. Personally, I realized how important these intense projects are in my life. The call to adventure is something I always look forward to and never decline. I realized that, in addition to the common goal, everyone was responsible for micro-missions, each one equally important and interdependent. Our collective success depended on our ability to individually accomplish our micro-missions."

MARIE-MICHÈLE FISET, PHYSIOTHERAPIST AND NAVIGATOR

"This experience made me realize how far you can go if you surround yourself with the right people. You can take 10 people who don't know each other, with different backgrounds and experiences, and form an exceptional team if you bring out the best in each of them. Thus, we can achieve extraordinary goals. I realized even more the value of human capital! Also, I realized through this adventure that I am where I should be professionally. What I love about my work as a physiotherapist is to team up with people and to help them reach their goals, whether it is to heal from an injury, to get back to recreational activities or to fulfil a dream. Obviously not everyone has the goal of being a RAAM finisher, but to be able to help my clients reach *their* 'RAAM,' their great goal, as I was able to help Sébastien, is an honor and a pleasure for me every day."

MARTIN PERREAULT, BIKE MECHANIC AND NAVIGATOR

"For me, the biggest success of our RAAM is the strength of our team. As someone who is quite independent and sometimes a bit anxious, I had fears and apprehensions about the group challenge that lay ahead. But instead, I discovered a family. Everyone was committed to our success, which brought efficiency, respect and a beautiful camaraderie. Personally, I learned to let go, to accept the uncertainty in front of me and to trust others. I believe I was able to contribute with my strengths, but also accept my weaknesses, and perhaps be a little less intense! I will always keep with me the many strong and memorable moments I experienced, thanks to the team."

ORPHÉ BEAUCHEMIN, DRIVER, RESPONSIBLE FOR ALL OF THE VEHICLES

"Beyond the remarkable feat that Sébastien achieved, this adventure was also a revealing experience about the importance of group cohesion to achieving a common mission. From the very first pedal strokes, Sébastien had already put in the hands of his team not merely the destiny of the race, but also his safety and health. In virtue of this demonstration of confidence and vulnerability, the team had no choice but to honor him. Today we can applaud Sébastien's physical and mental performance because of the cohesion and dedication of the team. It's thanks to the team and its unity that Sébastien can savor a well-deserved triumph."

PHILIPPE WAUTHIER, SPORTS DIRECTOR

"I think the first step to success was selecting the right team members. As far as teamwork goes, I give us a near-perfect score. The strategy of starting the weekly meetings early, involving people and the various team-building activities certainly had a major impact on the cohesion, motivation and cooperation in the team. Despite some less compatible personalities and unforeseen situations during the race, we managed to leverage everyone's strengths and to offset their weaknesses very well. Everyone was involved according to their abilities, and everyone gave their best. The project was a great human experience, and I hope our story will have a large-scale impact."

RÉJEAN LACHANCE, DRIVER, RESPONSIBLE FOR THE RV

"On the evening of March 18, 2022, at 6:20 p.m., when Sébastien asked me if I was interested in joining their team, I didn't hesitate one second to answer in the affirmative. Having known him for a decade, I knew that this would be, as he described it, 'the trip of a lifetime.' I met people with big hearts that I got to know quite well in a short period of time. They were all there for one purpose: to get to the finish line with a superhuman. Day and night, everyone took turns to make sure that Sébastien had everything he needed. No one counted their hours. Everyone gave 200 percent and believed in the mission. What touched me the most was to see us all supporting Sébastien so that he could succeed in this crazy race. It was truly the experience of a lifetime."

VALÉRIE BEAUDOIN-CARLE, SOCIAL MEDIA MANAGER AND DRIVER

"I come away from this experience with 10 new friends, but also with the knowledge that humans are phenomenally adaptable, and that with a lot of love, preparation and resilience, we are capable of accomplishing great things. It is a project that fills me with pride, for which I am grateful, and that left me with many precious memories. I was also lucky enough to jump into the adventure alongside my love, Gabriel. Sébastien's project also became Gabriel's project, and it was beautiful to see how he invested himself as if it were his own race. Gab, you inspire me! Your rigor, your discipline and your complete involvement really contributed to the success of this entire project!"

MY LAST WORDS

For me, Gabriel, RAAM was the experience of a lifetime. When I returned, I went through a period of withdrawal when I found myself alone in my office. It was as if a drug that kept me alive had been taken away from me. I thought long and hard about what made this drug so powerful and have come to the conclusion that it was the social connections I made with the team. Beyond the achievement and many lessons learned, my best memories are of all the little moments together. In the end, the true source of happiness is found in the quality of our relationships.

Many people dream of a prolific career that will allow them to achieve financial freedom and enjoy their retirement. Some dream of traveling the world and having unforgettable experiences, others dream of starting a family. Living in a way that is true to yourself, and not according to the expectations of others or society, brings a lot of happiness.

"Life is short, and you have to enjoy it." I like this philosophy, but I like this one even better: "Life is short and in order to make the most of it, you have to be brave every day."

As you may recall, before I committed to RAAM, I was hesitant. The experience made me realize that we should not wait passively for our next adventure; we must courageously create it.

CHAPTER 21

BEYOND ENGAGEMENT, THERE IS LOVE

Sébastien Sasseville

Our media campaign was a resounding success. We reached millions of people in Quebec and Canada through the numerous types of media coverage we received. I had the chance to be featured in the major media outlets in Québec, and in each interview, I spoke about the team and our collective success.

The success of this campaign relies heavily on the premise that it's not what you do that matters. It's the message, the meaning and the impact on others that really matters. The media liked our story because it meant something to so many people. In this regard, I know that our participation in RAAM has given a lot of hope to young people living with type 1 diabetes and their families.

As for me, once I got home, a long recovery process began. And contrary to what you might think, sleep doesn't come easy during the first few days after the race. My circadian rhythm was completely disrupted, and it took seven to 10 days to return to a normal sleep cycle.

During the first few days of rest, my insulin needs tripled. Inflammation, accumulated toxins and stress on the body create a lot of insulin resistance. Without going into detail, diabetes management continued to be a daily challenge upon our return.

As for my body, it slowly recovered. Ironically, the first few days were uneventful; it was after a few weeks that the bumps started to show. Back pain, knee pain and more. My immune system was weakened, so I was much more likely to get sick.

For a month I had a very good appetite and frequent cravings. I started RAAM at 175 pounds, finished at 170. Two months after returning, I was 188 pounds. I don't worry much about my weight, but I do keep an eye on it. My normal weight is around 180 pounds — a healthy weight that I can maintain with a normal level of physical activity and a good diet. After a big challenge, I always like to be a little heavier, to allow the body to recover properly.

I resumed some moderate physical activity about a month after my return. I started with swimming, light jogs and easy bike rides. I had been in a tight training structure for the last 10 years, so I really enjoyed to exercise just for fun for a summer.

WHAT'S NEXT?

If I had received a dollar for every time I was asked this question, I would be very rich!

The answer is I don't know. I loved RAAM; the challenge is tailor-made for me, as my great strength is endurance. With all that we learned, I am confident that we can go back and improve our performance. A few months after the adventure, I chose not to return the following year. I had the energy for the race but didn't have the will to sacrifice all my weekends and evenings for another year. It's the invisible part of these big projects that is the hardest. Getting to the starting line is often the biggest challenge.

It's also important to take enough time to digest the experience. Before jumping into the next adventure, it's good to step back and explore what you've learned and how the experience has transformed you. Despite a passion for these types of challenges, I find it important to continually validate my motivations. I need to make sure that the reasons I do these things are clear and that they are rooted in a strong mission.

Both from an individual and team perspective, it is essential to take breaks to step back and reflect. Is the destination still the right one? Am I doing what makes me happy? Are my actions consistent with my goals?

What do I need to change? Personally, I love the simple three-question formula popularized by the Netflix management team.*

- What should I start doing?
- What should I keep doing?
- What should I stop doing?

After RAAM, I said dozens of times that my plan was to not have a plan. The team remained skeptical, but for now, I am staying the course. In fact, after 15 years dedicated to big projects in sports, I want to have different experiences.

Many athletes experience difficult times after their professional sports career. We've all heard of Olympians experiencing depression after the Olympics. What causes this? In my opinion, it is very much a question of identity. We identify with our character as an athlete and find self-worth in it. I call it a pillar of our identity. The danger is to have only one pillar. When you remove that pillar, it's not surprising that one's identity shakes.

The more pillars our identity is based on, the less impact it has when you remove one pillar. For example, when a career-minded person has only one pillar to their identity — their job — a lost job or the transition to retirement may cause a period of darkness, a feeling of being lost or not knowing who they are anymore. The same thing happens when one's identity is only as a parent and the children leave the nest.

The more pillars a building has, the stronger it is. Work is one thing. We must have passions, hobbies, interests, different circles of friends and side projects. We are also spouses, friends, neighbors, relatives, colleagues. All these things are pillars that build our identity, and that we can lean on when we go through major life events.

SOMETHING EVEN BETTER THAN ENGAGEMENT

So what is left for me, Sébastien Sasseville? For a long time, I had the impression that after the project, I would owe a lifetime of debt to the team.

---

* MCCORD, Patty. How Netflix Reinvented HR. *Harvard Business Review*, 2014, vol. 92, no. 1, pp. 71-76.

A gift here, hours donated there, a letter of reference, a helping hand with a home project; let's just say that when one of the team members asks me for help, it's hard to say no!

However, one big lesson I learned is that not everything is an exchange.

Each member of the team had chosen to be there. They were all there for different reasons, and they were also there for something different. Helping others is one of the things that brings the most happiness to human beings. To feel that you are giving someone a hand, to feel that you are making a difference, to feel that you are enabling someone to rise up brings so much happiness that you don't need to receive anything in return.

I didn't have a debt to the team, I had a responsibility to continue to help others.

A leader gives without counting, without expecting anything in return. A leader gives so that others can be better, and so that the team can rise. I was lucky enough to be surrounded by 10 leaders.

Being the beneficiary of so much support, I learned that a leader must also know how to receive. I asked for help; I trusted; I surrounded myself with people who had skills that I did not have. For someone to give, someone must know how to receive.

I have grown as a human being thanks to Gabriel, Philippe, Valérie, Martin, Orphé, Manon, Réjean, Dan, Marc-Antoine and Marie-Michèle. Thank you, team, for trusting in me and believing in the mission. Thank you for having invested hundreds of hours in our project; thank you for having spent your precious vacation time at the race; thank you for your professionalism and your generosity. Thank you for giving your all, every day, until the last day.

To succeed in a difficult mission, human capital is the most important thing in the world. If you want to know how much human capital you have, go to war like I did, and you will see who will choose to follow you.

Gabriel and I wrote this book because we are proud. Both in preparation and execution, even though we were not CEOs of large companies, we felt like we were creating something worth telling.

I am a cyclist with type 1 diabetes, and I finished 12th in the world's toughest ultra-cycling race, 5th in my age group. I became the second type 1 diabetic in the race's 40-year history to finish RAAM in the solo category. This is quite an achievement.

Our team of volunteers, a group formed six months prior to the race, was made up of 10 individuals who mostly did not know each other. The challenge was daunting, and none of them had any experience supporting such an endeavour. This team was without a doubt one of the most cohesive and best prepared in 2022. Another big achievement.

Gabriel and I are proud to have brought together a group of talented individuals and guided them to create a highly engaged and top-performing team. When we started laying the groundwork for this book, teamwork was the main topic we identified. Then the word *engagement* started to emerge — a lot. After all, isn't engagement one of the main areas of focus in our organizations?

I always joke that, if you think about it, engagement is what happens when a leader convinces others to do the work he doesn't want to do! Engagement is good, but there's something better.

The highest level we must achieve in our teams is love. Our team created, cultivated and nurtured this ultimate state of cohesion, and I will keep this souvenir close to my heart for the rest of my life.

The goal became a calling that went beyond our roles, tasks and hours worked. We became a family and operated with a sense that no matter what happened, someone was always there for us. We developed a deep affection and caring for our teammates, for the mission and for the people we wanted to inspire. We all wanted to succeed, but only if it was together. It was because of this love that we accomplished the mission.

Now, it's your turn.

Team 661 at the finish line of the Race Across America 2022.

ACKNOWLEDGMENTS

Gabriel Renaud and Sébastien Sasseville

We would like to thank all those who, in one way or another, contributed to the success of our team and to the writing of this book.

All the members of team 661, without whom this experience would not have been possible: Philippe Wauthier, Valérie Beaudoin-Carle, Martin Perreault, Orphé Beauchemin, Manon Gauthier, Réjean Lachance, Dan Aponte, Marc-Antoine Legault-Frenette and Marie-Michèle Fiset.

Jennifer, and the whole team at ECW Press.

Erwan, and the whole team at Édito, our French editor.

Cliff Sherb, founder of Tristar Athletes, Sébastien's coach.

Charles Castonguay, Sébastien's physical trainer.

Daniel Renaud, co-founder of Hubu, for the team-building day before RAAM.

Patrick St-Martin, for driving the RV from Ottawa to Oceanside before the race.

The Race Across America organizers and volunteers.

Dominic Arpin and the film crew of the TV series *Les Crinqués*, for including our story.

Annie, Anne-Marie, Dominique, Daniel, Jocelyne, Elisabeth, Julie and Valérie, for the first revision of our manuscript.

ACKNOWLEDGMENTS

Dominique Moisan, for making the trip to Annapolis and bringing team members home.

Mireille, Alexandre and Lise-Anne, for taking care of Sébastien's cats during the race.

All the media outlets that have chosen to make our story shine.

Véronique Lavoie and Sophie Des Marais, for their support with our public relations.

Our sponsors, Lilly Canada, Dexcom and Tandem Diabetes Care.

Sundance Filardi, at the Spotlight Agency, for helping with sponsor relations.

Our gear sponsors, Tel-Loc, Spark Sports Nutrition, les cliniques PCN, Brave Vision, Lou Tec Saint-Romuald and Guru.

Our spouses and families, for their support throughout the project.

All those who liked and shared our publications on social networks to spread our message.

Thank you.

Sébastien Sasseville
www.sebinspire.com/en
seb@sebinspire.com

Sébastien Sasseville is one of the most accomplished endurance athletes in the world. His extraordinary accomplishments — which include the Race Across America, running across Canada and summiting Mount Everest — are made even more impressive by the fact that he lives with Type 1 Diabetes.

Transformed by his achievements and already a veteran motivational speaker with over 750 keynotes delivered in North America, Europe and Asia, including a TEDx talk, Sébastien is a globally recognized expert in Teamwork. He helps organizations to build the unwavering belief that they can achieve extraordinary results.

Sébastien Sasseville resides in Quebec City, Canada.

Gabriel Renaud
www.hubu.ca/en
gabriel@hubu.ca

Gabriel is a former collegiate hockey player and professional Ice Cross Downhill athlete with a background in neuroscience. Drawing from his experience in elite sports teams, Gabriel is the co-founder of Hubu, a company that specializes in team culture to build cohesive and high-performing teams.

Over the years, Hubu has carried out hundreds of workshops, keynotes and team events in Canada, the United States, Europe, Asia and Africa.

Gabriel Renaud resides in Quebec City, Canada.